IN THE
SHADOW
OF A
BADGE

IN THE SHADOW OF A BADGE

How I Discovered the Angels of 9/11
While Working with the FBI

LILLIE LEONARDI

HAY HOUSE

Australia • Canada • Hong Kong • India
South Africa • United Kingdom • United States

First published and distributed in the United Kingdom by:
Hay House UK Ltd, 292B Kensal Rd, London W10 5BE. Tel.: (44) 20 8962 1230;
Fax: (44) 20 8962 1239. www.hayhouse.co.uk

Published and distributed in the United States of America by:
Hay House, Inc., PO Box 5100, Carlsbad, CA 92018-5100. Tel.: (1) 760 431 7695 or
(800) 654 5126; Fax: (1) 760 431 6948 or (800) 650 5115. www.hayhouse.com

Published and distributed in Australia by:
Hay House Australia Ltd, 18/36 Ralph St, Alexandria NSW 2015. Tel.: (61) 2 9669 4299;
Fax: (61) 2 9669 4144. www.hayhouse.com.au

Published and distributed in the Republic of South Africa by:
Hay House SA (Pty), Ltd, PO Box 990, Witkoppen 2068. Tel./Fax: (27) 11 467 8904.
www.hayhouse.co.za

Published and distributed in India by:
Hay House Publishers India, Muskaan Complex, Plot No.3, B-2, Vasant Kunj, New Delhi
– 110 070. Tel.: (91) 11 4176 1620; Fax: (91) 11 4176 1630. www.hayhouse.co.in

Distributed in Canada by:
Raincoast, 9050 Shaughnessy St, Vancouver, BC V6P 6E5. Tel.: (1) 604 323 7100;
Fax: (1) 604 323 2600

A catalogue record for this book is available from the British Library.

ISBN 978-1-78180-108-6

Printed and bound in Great Britain by TJ International Ltd

MIX
Paper from
responsible sources
FSC
www.fsc.org   FSC® C013056

In thanksgiving to God, for illuminating my life's journey.

In gratitude to Archangel Michael and the legion of angels, for inspiring me to write this memoir.

CONTENTS

FOREWORD

Dear Dad,

I just wanted to take a moment and extend my deepest gratitude to you for all you did for me. You were an excellent father and friend. I am extremely grateful to you for all the gifts you gave us, your children and your family. You provided us with a wonderful mentor and taught us about love, life, integrity, and values. You inspired us to become the best we could be. You often told us that we children were your "gold and silver in this life." I hope you are looking down and seeing us shine in your light. You planted the seeds, and now you are watching us grow. We have grown into your mirror image. I hope you relish all our successes, for they are your legacy.

Also, I wanted to thank you for taking the time to teach me about God. You taught of God's endless love and forgiveness for His children. You preached that God continued to love us even in the times in our lives when we faltered and strayed from the path He had designed for us. You read us the stories of the Bible and provided insight into the wonders of God's mercy. You allowed us the opportunity to dream and hope for a better life. As a result of your teachings, on a fateful day more than ten years ago, I reached into the vast recesses of my soul and cried out to God for His help. Oh, and did He respond. God sent the world the gift of His angels. The angels I read about as a child and often believed that I saw. I *did* see them that day, in all of their brilliance and light. On September 11, 2001, God extended His hand and surrounded the world with his infinite love and guardianship. He sent His angels to protect those of us responding to the Pennsylvania crash site of Flight 93 and to gently carry the victims to His heavenly home. He provided passage and comfort to those who had sacrificed their lives in the name of honor. I was privileged to have observed the magnitude of His mercy and love.

I now release the story of Flight 93 and the field of angels in honor of my two fathers. In the worst moments of my life, I felt the presence of both my heavenly and earthly fathers' love, kindness, and patience. As you look down from Heaven, Dad, I hope you are proud. I hope that you smile and look around and say, "That's my daughter." For I look around on a continuous basis and say, "Look at all my father has bestowed upon me." I have been truly blessed.

Rest easy, Daddy. I'll see you when I see you. . . .

PREFACE

When I look at people, I witness the internal source of their being, not the external truth of the person. I see the purity that is derived from their spirit buried within the caverns of their bodies and connected to their minds.

This was always a problem for me because I wanted to see the enlightened soul of one and all. Yet this insight was in direct conflict with the career I had chosen. As a law enforcement professional, I had to learn to lead with my mind, not my heart. To trust my primal instincts, not my emotional responses. If I was to survive in this new world of policing, I quickly needed to become less trusting of my fellow human beings and more calculating as I learned to immediately evaluate the person in front of me.

Living in these two different worlds, I spent much time not acknowledging my true self. It was a lifestyle that nearly shattered my life. (The doctors who later treated me for post-traumatic stress disorder wondered how my mind had survived.) But more precious than that, this split almost cost the loss of my heart and soul.

This dichotomy may also explain my two-dimensional writing style. One style is formatted from the linear side of my brain, authored in a straightforward and direct manner—think of the many police reports I've written. It is through this lens that I perceived my world of policing, its contexts and effects. The pages that follow will unfold in a similar way, very clear and precise. This is the first voice of who I am, and thus the one you will hear most often as you read the chapters of this book.

The second writing style is more poetic. I am told it is flowery in its design. It mirrors the voice of my heart and soul, and so delivers to the reader a glimpse of the inner sanctum I hold closest. As I write in this second mode, I can hear it, feel it, and see it as I type. The words have a life of their own and pass easily from pen to paper. It is as if some being has taken hold of my inner creativity and set it free. My muses come to life, and my spirit soars as I write.

As I wrote this book, it became clear why my mind has been so convoluted in these last years. I have been living with one foot firmly planted on the earth and the other soaring in an ethereal domain. I've lived in two separate and distinct worlds that, over time, became so entwined it was virtually impossible for my mind to function.

Authoring these chapters has helped integrate these two parts of me, bringing my life to a point of healing and evolution. Living in two worlds, I almost drove myself to destruction. The writing has prompted a better understanding of myself and the inner workings of my heart, mind, and soul. It has made me keenly aware that there is no longer a need to live in varying worlds; I can instead intertwine the two and live as one.

The following chapters relate how, in the wake of 9/11, these two worlds collided. That collision set the stage for the transformation of my soul. The story details aspects of my life as I lived it. Shadowed by a badge—the badge I'd worn first as a police officer. In telling this story, there is no longer a need to stay hidden behind that metal shield. It is time for me to step out. To allow my soul to shine forth again. And to allow the truth in my heart to illuminate my life and my journey.

Samuel Corey

On that day, I saw a vision of an archangel laying down his sword and embracing his heart. I took it to symbolize the metamorphosis of humanity to the higher level of spirituality. The warrior was beckoned to lay down his weapon and move toward the light and love of an open heart.

CHAPTER

1

A DAY OF INFAMY: SEPTEMBER 11, 2001

September 11, 2001, began as any late summer day in western Pennsylvania. The weather held the promise of being clear, bright, and hot. It was the time of the year that I looked forward to: the heat of the day, the cool crisp nights, and the changing color of the leaves dangling from the trees. Seasonal changes always seemed to lift my mood. The early days of September were a busy time with work, too. The month brought the beginning of a new school year. As the Community Outreach Specialist for the Pittsburgh Division of the Federal Bureau of Investigation (FBI), much of my day would focus on prevention and intervention programming in the numerous school districts within my jurisdiction.

This particular day had already been filled with preparations for work. Being a creature of habit, I had an early morning routine that included drafting notes for that day's meetings and other activities. I had already documented the initial information needed to compose the daily reports. This information was used to compile the monthly—and a portion of the biannual—reports for review by FBI management. The biannual report provided an overall picture of all the projects the Pittsburgh Field Office engaged in as part of the extensive Community Outreach Program (COP).

The Pittsburgh Field Office COP had received a great deal of recognition, both for the initiatives we developed and the external partnerships we established. Our outside partnerships were vast and included representation from federal, state, and local government; law enforcement agencies; child protective services; community and youth-based groups; nonprofit organizations; school districts; and elected officials.

As coordinator and manager of the program, I was very proud of the collaboration and accomplishments of COP's external partners. Each was very dedicated to their "call to service." All worked in tandem to address, intervene, respond to, and resolve any problematic issues in the cities and schools. More specifically, we all united to prevent and decrease the violence and crime plaguing our communities. Our collaborative team worked to help eliminate issues such as drug and alcohol abuse, gang violence, street crime, and any other problems that arose.

Addressing the needs of children was our primary focus, and it was always the work that gave me greatest pleasure. Through our prevention and intervention programs, developed and conducted in partnership with so many amazing people, the youth received much-needed guidance. Many of the agency representatives were directly involved in mentoring, and we all worked tirelessly in the best interest of our children.

As I went outside that morning, the warmth of a brilliant sun greeted me. Standing on the front porch, draped in sunlight, the brilliant rays flooded through me and lifted my spirit. I stood there for a moment or two, just breathing in the fresh air and admiring the beauty of the day.

I walked the short distance to my bureau-owned vehicle (known in my circle of colleagues as a "Bucar") and attempted to start it. To my surprise, the engine would not turn over. As limited as my knowledge about mechanics was, I deduced that the battery was dead. At that point, I became frustrated. I knew I would be late for my first meetings of the day. Muttering a few curse words, I got out of the car, called the field office to alert my supervisor of the problem, and contacted the division's on-duty mechanic. The mechanic informed me that he would be out to tow the vehicle into the garage in about an hour's time.

I went back inside and began making telephone calls to cancel my morning appointments. With each conversation, I became increasingly agitated. I am generally on time, and I dislike rescheduling meetings. As I awaited the arrival of the mechanic, I turned on ABC's *Good Morning America;* the least I could do was get caught up on the early news of the day. I gazed at the television screen, seeing what appeared to be footage of a plane striking a tall building in New York City. I remember wondering if this was a preview from some upcoming television show or a dramatic movie trailer. Just then I heard Diane Sawyer say that ABC had just received confirmation that the plane had indeed struck one of the Twin Towers in Downtown Manhattan.

As the news of the plane and a live shot of the tower appeared on the screen, the story of 9/11 began to unfold. Instinctively, my background in policing kicked in. I knew the incident was not an accident; it was an intentional act. Who, I wondered, had perpetrated such a heinous crime? All of my years of police training did not prepare me for the events that the world would witness that morning. I watched as the camera stayed fixed on the first tower. I was terrified by the sight of the large gaping hole in the upper floors of the building. Glass and steel had exploded, sending remnants of the structure crashing to the pavement below. The tower became a burning inferno, its black smoke and orange flames in dramatic contrast to the quiet morning sky. It looked like some ancient volcano on the verge of an eruption, ready to wreak havoc on the streets of New York City.

I was transfixed. But just as my mind began to settle, the second plane flew toward Tower Two. It struck the building with such blunt force that human survival seemed impossible. Each of the subsequent events flashing on the television screen appeared more horrific than the last. Inside the towering infernos, victims began jumping from the windows. My heart ached for each of them and for the choice they felt forced to make. My thoughts strayed to their families. How would they feel if they recognized their loved one plunging toward death? How would they ever be able to erase from their minds that last agonizing glimpse?

The fire now appeared to have a life of its own. The next scenes were those of the emergency response vehicles racing to the towers. The newsreels showed hundreds of vehicles parking in front of the towers. Once parked, the emergency response personnel rushed into the buildings' entrances. As uniformed men and women ran inside the towers and disappeared from view, I wondered if they realized they might not survive. In their attempt to save the lives of others, I thought, they may themselves become the tertiary victims of this horrific event.

My mind flashed back to the moments in my own career as a police officer. How often had duty required me to aid or resolve a difficult situation? Memories of my days wearing blue filtered through my mind: my thoughts, my responses, the mind-set that would take hold of my being. A familiar mechanism would click on in my head, as my training kicked into gear. It all surfaced as I watched the towers ablaze.

When I talk about this "mechanism," I'm hard-pressed to explain what I mean. It's not a sensation or a feeling, but more of a mechanical occurrence that prompts a particular reaction from me. Many who wear "the blue" talk about this response. For me, it was a learned confidence—a knowing—that came from extensive training at the academy and in my first years as a police officer.

In retrospect, I believe I always had this mechanical ability. Even as a child, if something bad happened—if one of my siblings was injured, for example—I was ready and willing to aid them. The amount of blood or whether someone was crying in pain didn't matter; I looked past my fear and responded as needed. My younger siblings would feel so much better if I was with them after they were hurt. On many occasions, I would hold one of them in my arms as Mom drove the car to the hospital. My presence seemed to quiet their fears. Even now, when something bad happens, my daughter often says: "If the world is falling apart, you want Mom to help. She always knows what to do."

Her response wasn't always so positive. In my days as a police officer, my daughter would call me "Robocop."

It was her way of describing what happened when this mechanism kicked in. My daughter, now in her 40s, tells me that a transformation would take place whenever I put on my uniform. Something would take hold of me, a kind of trance that seemed to erase any essence of humanity. I was no longer her mother, but some robotic persona. She claimed my demeanor would change, that I even walked and talked differently. There were times when she would say to me, "Hey, Robocop, my mom is missing. I want to file a report. When you find her, will you ask her to come home, because I miss her."

At first, I took great offense at my daughter's words. They sounded so harsh and disrespectful, and they unnerved some part of me. But as time went on, I realized she was speaking the truth all too clearly. Back then, I was not aware of the change in my personality—so I was certainly not capable of accepting it. But as I reflect now, I realize that she was right. I did have an alter ego—an identity that kicked into gear when I wore that uniform—that was separate and distinct from my true essence.

Moreover, my femininity seemed to dissipate each time I buttoned the starched shirt of my uniform and placed that badge over my heart. As a police officer, I was not supposed to let my feelings get in the way—a rule that was especially important as a woman on a male-dominated force. The badge was more a cue for my unfeeling, robotic persona to come to the surface than a shield to protect my heart. It became a symbol for hiding my true feelings, for burying them deep in some cavern inside me. It was there to shield me from the pain of all the negative events I would witness in my years on the force.

My heart became shielded from emotional responses—responses that were replaced by the "mechanism." As I received a call for service, it was as if a tiny clicking sound would ring in my ear. With the first click, I focused my attention on the situation. All of the details would filter through my mind. With the second click, my mind would center on their actions. A sort of tunnel vision would take hold. With the third click, my mind determined the action necessary for my response. And, with the fourth and final click, my mind and body sprang into action. As the mechanism switched on, so did the transfer of my behavior. It was not necessary for me to shed my glasses like Clark Kent as he switched from the mild-mannered reporter to Superman. No, it took little conscious effort on my part to become "Robocop"; to fine-tune my mind in preparedness to respond and survive. The experience was primal. My instincts heightened in order to protect my life and those of others, if necessary.

As my mind refocused on the events of that September day—incidents of such magnitude—I was saddened for the responding officers who would be required to stir up great energy and courage. I prayed for their well-being and for their guardian angels to protect and guide them as they moved through the burning buildings in search of survivors and victims alike.

It was just then that Diane Sawyer announced a third plane had struck the Pentagon outside Washington, D.C., and much of the city was being evacuated. She indicated there was suspicion of a fourth plane involved in this plot, but its whereabouts and destination were as yet unknown. Minutes later, the news of a plane crashing in a remote field in western Pennsylvania echoed across the television screen.

Each of these incidents followed the other, as if staged in a movie. The cumulative impact would soon be heard and felt around the world. A new generation of young Americans would identify themselves with these heinous events, just as mine had identified with the Vietnam War and my parents' generation had identified with World War II and Pearl Harbor.

As I listened to the news, I wondered what was next. Almost immediately, I watched in disbelief as the towers began to crumble under the heat of the flames. I heard the once mighty towers scream in a thunderous roar at the strength of the fire within. I felt the same horror I could see in the faces of the victims running away from the scene. Those of us who witnessed the carnage via our television screens could not help but feel the same deep emotions in the recesses of our souls. I felt immobilized and helpless as I watched New York City and its inhabitants become paralyzed with fear. Thousands of bystanders were unable to help their fellow human beings. People were panicking and running to save their lives as the remnants of the towers came raining down upon them.

From my perspective, the crumbling towers, with their smoke and white powder moving in every direction, resembled a great tsunami that was about to swallow all in its path. The faces of the innumerable people affected by the morning's events—the news media, the emergency responders, the random victims, and even that of President Bush as he sat in contemplation at an elementary school in Florida—appeared as a kaleidoscope in my mind's eye.

A deep sense of pain began to churn inside me as I watched the television. And, like most others viewing, I cried for those who had been lost and injured. My heart wept, my tears fell, and I knelt upon the floor. My prayers began to flow, and I heard my voice softly whisper to

God for His aid. The aftermath of bewilderment began to take hold as I sat glued to the television and wondered, *What next?*

My first impulse was one of parental concern. Was my daughter, who worked for the United States Attorney's Office in downtown Pittsburgh, safe? Was my granddaughter, who was in her first days of kindergarten, being protected? Where was the rest of my family, and were they all right? How could I protect them? Would there be any more attacks? How could I help? I called my daughter. She was safe but afraid. She began to cry and asked questions about what she should do. I told her that I loved her and she should take every precaution for her safety. She should follow the direction of the building's security officer and find a safe passage home. As she asked more questions, I felt my maternal instinct arise. Although I had just seen her earlier that morning, my heart ached to put my arms around her and soothe away her fear. As my mind raced between my need to reassure her and my intent to get moving, I reiterated my love for her. I told her to be careful and to take great care of herself and my granddaughter. I told her not to worry, because I fully trusted that God would see all of us through this crisis. And I told her that if for some reason I didn't get to see her again, she should remember I dearly loved both her and the little one. I ended the conversation by saying, "Even when I'm gone, you'll know that I'm near each time the wind blows through your hair. When the wind moves, imagine my hand is resting on your head and listen as my voice whispers the comforting words you need to hear. I'll never be too far away."

As I spoke these words, I realized that my paternal grandmother had told me a similar story about herself and our eternal connection to each other. My grandmother had often explained that even after her death she would always be near. She would appear in the form of a dove. Each and every time I saw a dove, she told me, it should remind me that she is present in my life. Now, in my moment of need, I wished for the appearance of a dove and the presence of my grandmother, too. I dearly needed a sign to indicate some form of comfort was near.

As I hung up the phone with my daughter, I wondered how many other mothers would connect with their children in the moments following this event. How many others would not be able to reach their children or, tragically, never hear the voice of their own dear child again? I remember saying a prayer and thanking God for the opportunity to have been able to hear my daughter's voice. I prayed for her protection, for that of my grandchild, and for the rest of my family. I prayed for those who were injured or killed and for strength to serve my community.

With that, my mind began to shift from that of a mother, grandmother, daughter, and sister to that of a law enforcement officer. I immediately contacted the Pittsburgh Division's communication desk and was advised to stand by because the office was awaiting orders from FBI headquarters. I then contacted a division administrator and immediately volunteered my services to respond to Shanksville or any of the other sites where help might be needed. I was told to report to the office because staff members were needed to respond to the Shanksville site to set up a mobile command and help arrange the necessary ancillary services to prepare for an all-agency response.

THE RACE TOWARD DESTRUCTION

I ran from my home and jumped into my personal vehicle. I felt like a television superhero leaping into a car and preparing to respond to some crime perpetrated by an unknown villain. I raced through traffic to the field office. I was oblivious to the movement of traffic or the speed of my car. As my foot pressed harder on the gas pedal, tunnel vision began to take hold. My mind became transfixed on the mission ahead. I needed to get to the FBI office as swiftly as possible.

In my car, I once again assumed the role I had played as a patrol officer some 17 years before. As my thoughts raced, I recalled my first high-speed chase. I remembered the sensations of my breathing and the fight-or-flight response surging through my body. The fear erupting inside me, feeding the raw adrenaline as it coursed through my veins, creating a singular focus: to stop the threat ahead. The words *drive, drive, drive* echoed through my mind. It was the voice of my amygdala, of my brain ordering and preparing me for battle.

My tunnel vision remained on the image of that first car chase—how I'd maneuvered each turn. My immediate focus, however, stayed on the road ahead and on the 20-odd miles yet to travel. I felt no emotion. I felt only the clicking of the "mechanism," all too familiar to me from my past life as a cop.

With each click, I felt a restrained, calculated calm begin to set in. It was a calming sensation that was drilled into me and each of my fellow cadets, day after day in the early days at the Police Academy. This familiar feeling meant only one thing: my entire being was preparing for the unknown battle ahead. The training took hold, and the law enforcement officer emerged. My true self slipped away, overtaken by the Robocop personality known all too well to my family. The loving daughter, mother, granddaughter, sister, and friend fell away, and the seasoned veteran of the street emerged. I had heard the "call of the wild," and the warrior in me had responded. The transformation to the robotic trance now begun, survival became the paramount issue at hand. The old familiar robotic stance had gained control of me and would stay intact for the next 12 days.

When I arrived at the office, there were people scurrying in every direction. My colleagues were geared up and readying the command post for action. The command post would become the epicenter of all activity. It would be the location where all major decisions were made, the "hub" where the field office administrators would receive the orders generated from the FBI higher echelon in Washington, D.C. The command post would be operated on a 24/7 schedule with three shifts of personnel working around the clock. Since I had called ahead and spoken to an administrator, I was immediately requested to assist two other employees in transporting mobile command to the Shanksville crash site. I agreed to accompany these employees and work in any capacity needed.

As I left the building, I realized I was about to enter a domain I would have hoped never to see. I questioned my ability to accomplish the tasks that would need to be addressed. But in the few minutes it took to drive to the offsite garage, I stilled my mind and began to hear the familiar clicking echo inside my head once again. It didn't take long to arrive at the off-site garage where the mobile command unit was parked. All too soon I pulled into the ramp of the metal structure. I spent the next few minutes hastily assisting other employees as they prepared the unit for the trip northeast to Shanksville. When the vehicle was ready for departure, we were provided with an escort by the Pennsylvania State Police (PSP) to help us move through the now-snarled traffic of downtown Pittsburgh. There were vehicles traveling in every direction. The cars looked meshed, like a finely woven spiderweb.

I saw many hurried pedestrians crossing the streets in between the cars and crosswalks. There were hundreds of people at the bus stops, eagerly awaiting transportation that would take them home to their families and a safe place to hide.

Although the traffic was jammed in every direction, the drivers seemed more considerate than usual. Cars gave way for others to enter the road, including us. The egress was slow but systematic. It was as if the vibration of human nature had been changed. It was as if routine road rage had dissipated when the first plane slammed into the tower. People now seemed to have an ability to comprehend the levels of travesty not understood before this day. The balance of life had changed, shifting from self-preservation to empathy for our fellow man.

While each face we passed was different from the next, they all shared the same look: a look of fear of the unknown. It was a look I fully understood; we were all wearing it that day. The look resonated in the pit of my soul on 9/11 and remains there for posterity. I stared into the crowd, wishing desperately to catch a glimpse of my daughter. She was not there. I only hoped she was safely on her way home.

The trip to the remote landfill took approximately 90 minutes. In that time, my mind raced with questions. What would the scene hold? Would there be any survivors? If there were, what shape would they be in? Had the scene been secured? Was there any hope for the mothers who were waiting to find out if their children had been aboard Flight 93? Was I prepared for the momentous task ahead of me and the initial responders? Deep inside of me one of the questions was answered. I had taken an oath some 17 years before to protect and serve my community. This day, more than any in my career, would determine for me if I would be capable of living up to that oath.

A FIELD OF ANGELS: SHANKSVILLE

As our team neared the location of the Shanksville crash site, the trooper driving our escort vehicle provided the necessary credentials for passage through the state police roadblocks. Barriers had been stationed over an eight-mile radius in order to protect the scene. I again wondered what the crime scene would hold. If the scene was eight miles in diameter, there would be much to consider and plan. All of us had a grueling task ahead.

As we neared the crash site, we saw that the fire personnel—with all their trucks and equipment—were leaving. They had finished extinguishing the fire that had been ignited by the plane's jet fuel. As we drove past their vehicles, I glanced at the many faces of the firefighters perched on their seats and ladders. It was as if I could see the same glimpse of despair in each set of eyes. In that moment I realized that none of us was alone in our quest to serve. It was a comforting thought but one that chilled me to the bone. If we were truly not alone, how could such a devastating incident take place? With all our care, how could we not have prevented this travesty? It's a question that still haunts me to this day, one I ponder all too frequently.

As we left the safety of our vehicle, we began to walk the area of the crash site. The thick smells of fuel, burning wood, and smoldering pine hung low in the air, burning my nose and lungs. It was hard to breathe.

It was then that I was reminded of my early days as a novice cop—and the first time I smelled the odor of death. It is a scent one never forgets. I was called to the home of an elderly man who hadn't been heard from in several days. His family and neighbors had made repeated attempts to contact him and were worried about his safety. As my partner and I walked onto the front porch that warm summer day, I caught an unfamiliar scent. It wouldn't take long to learn from the veteran officer that this was the smell of death.

When we entered the house, the odor was so intense that it took everything in me not to lose my dinner. It raced into my nostrils and lingered there. My partner handed me a small jar of Vicks VapoRub and told me to smear a little under my nose. He explained that using the rub would help block the smell. I dipped my finger into the tiny blue container and retrieved a dab of the rub, smearing it at the openings of my nostrils and across my upper-lip area. The familiar smell of eucalyptus soon permeated my nose, allowing me to focus on the task at hand.

I had been to many a crime scene in my former career as a cop, but nothing had ever prepared me for that field in

Pennsylvania. As I surveyed the scene, I felt my heart shatter into a billion pieces. The pain in the depths of my chest was such that I could barely catch my breath. My stomach turned, and I felt my soul stir in anguish.

In 14 years as a police officer, I had witnessed many malicious acts. My first big case was an armed robbery at the local state store—my first glimpse into the criminal mind. It had been my proving ground, my reminder of the importance of gathering the evidence. In crime solving, it doesn't matter what crime has been perpetrated. The scene usually contains an enormous amount of physical evidence. There are weapons, bloodstains or spatters, DNA, fingerprints, broken windows, or severely damaged vehicles left behind. This evidence must be gathered to provide the necessary information to solve the crime. Evidence helps answer the questions of who, what, when, where, and why. But at this scene, the old adage "ashes to ashes and dust to dust" immediately came to mind.

On this day the crime scene was unique. Not because the field was filled with carnage—the direct opposite. What evidence remained was scattered in every direction. I was deeply disturbed. Where was the plane? Where were the bodies? Where were the remnants to remind us that these people had existed? It was as if all these lives had been scattered to the wind.

I felt tears well up. I tried to keep them from falling; I didn't want the others to see me cry. I didn't want the "female" in me to escape and appear weak in some way. But I couldn't hold back the tears. I tasted them, and they were bitter and salty. My tears reflected the way I was feeling. I was deeply saddened by the events of the day. I was angry at the act of violence that had been perpetrated on this field. As I heard my inner voice scream in agony,

I whispered, "How could anyone justify killing others in God's name?"

The God I knew would never have expected me to kill or commit an act of this nature. The God of my Bible stories had promoted the love of man. He had forgiven us in parable after parable. Where had the Bible indicated that killing was required to gain entrance to Heaven? The Bible teaches us to love one another, not to destroy one another. Whose interpretation of the holy word would permit such behavior?

The God I knew would never call for men to kill for His sake. The God I had read about in my youth was one of love and kindness. After all, hadn't he given us His only son for the betterment of all humankind? Hadn't He taught us to love and cherish others? To turn the other cheek when need be? He wanted us to live in peace and harmony with one another.

My heart had broken in these first minutes at the scene and would remain broken for many years to come. Any innocence I'd retained over the years dissipated as I stepped onto that field. My body heaved a great sigh, and I felt the purest part of me retreat into hiding. It did not want to see what lay before me.

Debris was scattered as far as the eye could see, on the ground as well as in the trees. I couldn't tell if what we were looking at were human remains, or if we'd ever be able to recover any of the poor souls who had perished on the plane. Those of us on site could see that a portion of the plane had embedded itself into the ground. The cockpit had sunk into the soft landfill, and the ground had swallowed it up as in ceremonial response to the tragedy. Remnants of the plane lay in bits of cinder, like a fragile balsa-wood plane that had been set on fire. The forest was blackened and scarred by the events of the morning. I peered at the scene. A whole new era of terrorism had just erupted and swept across our land. And we had just walked into a moment that would forever mark this generation and this new millennium.

I recall looking at the faces of the other FBI and the Federal Aviation Administration (FAA) personnel. I felt as if we were all moving in slow motion. Once again, I remembered my life as a police officer—all the moments spent patrolling the streets and responding to incident after incident. At times, during the heat of some scuffle, life would begin to move in slow motion. It was as if my mind needed to slow down to remember every detail, to record the event mentally and emotionally.

It was midafternoon, and the sun was at its peak. I could feel it on my face, but it lent no comfort. We were standing in the middle of the forest, but there were no sounds of birds or other animals, no stirring of a wind. There was only a calm silence giving way to an eerie feeling. The feeling I was experiencing felt similar to when I prayed. It felt as if we had stepped onto hallowed ground, a sacred place only a privileged few would get to experience. In this moment of silence, I knew I was experiencing one of those events that forever changes a human being. I sensed an epiphany. Once again, I began to pray for those lost, for their parents and families, for those of us here to assist, and for those who were on their way to the scene.

As we moved across the field, I walked in the same way I would walk at a cemetery. So many lives had been lost on this ground. I was careful and deliberate, so as not to disturb some unseen presence. I walked over to a small rise in the ground and attempted to survey the entire scene. I wanted to grasp the magnitude of the event and our task.

As I looked across the immense space of the scene, I saw a shimmer of light by my left shoulder. The light flickered at first, playing against that of the sun. The light reminded me of my first trip to Ireland, when I had seen a large school of salmon swimming very close to the water's edge. The light of their scales had merged with that of the sun and sent brilliant crystal shimmers across my view. I remember that the light was mesmerizing, and many of us stood witness to it. It was an amazing moment for me.

On the field, the shimmer of light began to grow off to my left until it was almost blinding. I turned and looked at it more directly, and it began to evolve into a foggy white mist. The mist then began to move, swirling in patterns of spectacular white light. Then, before my eyes, the mist took shape. To my amazement, there at the left of the crash site stood what appeared to be a legion of angels.

There were hundreds of them, standing in columns— a field of angels, emerging from the realms of the mist. I recognized them as archangels, wings arched up toward the sky. Each of them appeared to be dressed in warrior garments, like a legion of Roman centurions from centuries past. They were standing vigil, gazing at the surrounding perimeter. The looks on their faces were intense yet gentle. Calming. They stood like soldiers guarding their ground in preparation for the next battle. They appeared ready to receive the next command from their leader. And they clearly had a leader—for he stood majestically in front of them all.

This archangel stood with confidence, radiance, and an aura of leadership. The saber in his hand angled toward the ground in resting mode. I knew instantly this had to be Michael, for in my Catholic upbringing the Archangel Michael had always been depicted as the warrior. He was also known as the guardian of law enforcement.

These celestial beings were so numerous that their features began to blend together. The pureness of their beauty—and the radiant light surrounding them—was overwhelming to me. Each was unique, and all were beautiful. I marveled at the image of these lovely creatures. They looked just as they were depicted in the frescoes Michelangelo painted in the Sistine Chapel some 500 years ago.

As I gazed at the angels, my mind slowed its pace. I paused at each new motion they made. With each movement, a detail was forever etched in my memory. It was as if there were a sketch artist inside my mind's eye preserving all the minute details with an indelible pen.

The moment was reminiscent of my first big case as a police officer. My sergeant had requested that I assist him with an armed robbery investigation. The suspect was accused of robbing the local liquor store. Although the victims had provided a very accurate accounting of the events and had supplied an excellent description of the perpetrator, there were no fingerprints to link a known criminal to the case. As part of the investigation, a forensic artist had sketched a likeness of the suspect. Since there was no person identified as the actual suspect, a "John Doe" warrant was issued. A John Doe warrant is a document that permits a police officer access to any known criminal—or any person—fitting the description or the sketch.

I was excited about the opportunity to assist in the case and grateful for the chance to prove myself. A few months into the investigation, however, there were still no leads. Then, one cold wintry night, we hit a home run. During a routine patrol on the midnight shift, I passed a car with four males riding in it, two in the front and two in the back. The car was traveling in the opposite direction from me, but I caught a glimpse of the male sitting in the rear passenger seat. Within seconds, my mind clicked to the still image of the sketch from the armed robbery. I radioed for backup, and within minutes two other police officers were on the scene. We flipped on the emergency lights and headed back in the direction of the car. We pulled it over and conducted a traffic stop. As each of the passengers was requested to identify himself, the male in question kept pulling his knitted ski cap farther down over his face. When asked to give his name and produce some form of identification, he became belligerent and questioned all of us about the stop. One of the officers asked him to step away from the vehicle. At that point I was sure the man standing in front of us matched the sketch. He was placed under arrest and transported to the holding cell.

My eye for detail had proven valuable. The man we arrested bore a very close resemblance to the sketch obtained from the victimized liquor-store employees. Within a short time, the suspect was identified, arraigned, and held without bail. A few months later he was convicted on the charges and incarcerated.

I knew then that my gift for detail would be helpful in my chosen profession. And on 9/11, it would prove to be a gift. Thanks to it, I was able to memorize the vision of the angels standing on the field. Over the next years, in spite of many ups and downs, my memory sustained each and every detail of those first minutes at the crash site—and of the angels who showed themselves to me there.

Back on the field, however, I tried to shake the image of the angels. I thought I was losing my grip on reality. I remember telling myself that, once again, my imagination had begun to play tricks on my mind. But my trained eye stayed fixated on the image of the angelic visitors and the other faces that appeared to be a part of the entourage.

I wondered if this was my mind's way of calming me, in preparation for the task ahead.

In some ways I was the least likely person to see angels. But in another way, it made sense. I had always believed in angels; my Catholicism had taught me to. My father and I had many a discussion about guardian angels and their purpose. Over the years, I believed I had seen angels. I had seen them quite often as a child and had shared this information with my father prior to his death. And as an adult, especially since my father's death in 1994, I had been visited by an archangel. Known to me as Michael, he always came in my time of need. But he had never before appeared quite in the form that now presented itself on this field.

The voice inside my soul—a voice I had heard so often—told me that the angels were real. It whispered in my ear that the archangels were there to serve and protect those souls who had sacrificed their lives for the well-being of others. They were there to escort the heroes of Flight 93 to Heaven. Additionally, the angels had come to protect those of us who would play a part in the investigation of this act of terror.

I tried to shake the words from my mind because I needed to focus on the task at hand.

At that moment, the FAA ordered all of us off the field, as the forest had reignited. Also, there were hazardous materials on the ground upon which we were walking, and we needed to be concerned for our own health. I began to move back toward the mobile command unit. I moved like a robot off the field, unable to respond and think about anything but the vision I had just observed. I remember I heard what I thought was the shriek of a hawk. I turned and saw the predatory bird swooping down over the exact location where the angels had stood. It was the first animal

23

sound I had heard since our arrival on the field. I looked again at the hawk and saw that all the angels had now disappeared. Only the light of the brilliant sun remained. I recall praying to God to give me a sign to confirm that the vision of the angels had truly happened, that it hadn't just been an apparition. Had He given me a marvelous gift and blessing, or had I merely imagined so, for my own comfort?

My prayer was soon answered. In front of me, I saw a Bible lying on the ground. It lay on the sandy soil all alone, away from any other remnants of the crash. It was in full view for three of us to see. One of my colleagues even commented on it. To my amazement, the Bible was completely intact. The only damage was that it was singed around the edges. All at once, the wind began to blow for the first time that day. As the wind whipped around us, it caused the pages of the Bible to blow open. The Bible opened to Psalm 23, "The Lord Is My Shepherd." In that moment, I knew God was giving me the sign I had requested. It was confirmation of a miracle—a wonderful vision of His archangels on this field of glory. God had provided me with an opportunity that few would be privileged enough to observe in their lifetime. Little did I know at the time how ill-prepared I was to share my story of amazing grace. It would take a long time before I was able to do so.

CHAPTER

4

THE FIRST FEW DAYS AT THE CRASH SITE

I spent the next two days caught up in a frenzy of activity, as did most others who were working at the crash site. In a perpetual state of hypervigilance, I helped with the coordination of the ancillary services. I drove an all-terrain vehicle around the landfill and delivered personnel, messages, equipment, water, food, and other items needed to help prepare for the huge recovery endeavor that was about to take place.

The tasks were varied and unending. Our job descriptions didn't matter anymore; everyone was willing to assist in any way that was needed. As I stood back and watched the others at work, the flurry of activity reminded me of a busy beehive in action. Although each bee worked to achieve its individual task, they also assisted one another to meet the needs of the entire community. It was the same for all of us. We worked in tandem to address each problem as it arose, all while recovering the remnants that were strewn about the dusty landfill.

Each night I traveled back to my home, only to awaken in the morning for the journey back to the crash site. I was totally exhausted. The long days at the site and the late-night drives home were sapping my energy and adding to the daily stress. The round trip averaged about 150 miles a day. I rarely arrived home before midnight. With only a few hours of sleep, I would be back on the road at 6:30 A.M. in order to report to the site by 8:00 A.M.

Those first two nights were tough on my body, mind, and soul. Returning home each night, my ability to turn off my feelings was tested. The isolation of remaining firm and in my "law-enforcement zone" took every bit of extra energy I possessed. I had to remind myself continually that staying in "the zone" was necessary to my survival. In this time of high anxiety, it became increasingly hard to maintain control of my emotions, especially with my daughter and granddaughter living with me.

The two of them had been in my home for about five years, since my granddaughter had been nine months old. My daughter had requested to move back in with me because her relationship with the little one's father had not gone well. As she and her live-in boyfriend parted ways, I was eager to provide a refuge for her and her child. I knew it would give me a better chance to know my new grand-child. So without any hesitation, I purchased a lovely red-brick home just a couple of blocks away from my mother's house, right across the street from one of my brothers. It was the ideal location for the three of us. With my hectic schedule and traveling, I knew it would be comforting for my daughter to have relatives nearby. If for any reason she needed help when I was not available, there were family members who could step in.

After my divorce I'd spent much of my time alone. I hadn't realized just how lonesome I had been until the first night after their arrival. As I peeked into their bedroom late that night, I felt my heart twist at the sight of their sleeping faces. Once again, my maternal instincts were engaged. My girls were back home! I welcomed the chance to become even closer to them.

But now, as I walked into our home late each night, I found their presence extremely heart wrenching. It now had a reverse effect on my heart. I felt an even stronger need to be with them—to find a way to assure their safety and security. I longed for their touch, to hear their laughter and their voices. I desperately needed the comfort of my family. But I also knew that if I allowed myself to feel my love for them—to feel the humanity they inspired in me—I would have a hard time returning to my focused, trancelike state at the site. As painful as it was, it was best that the girls were sleeping each night when I returned home. My body and mind were very tired, and my limited energy needed to be reserved to complete my job requirements.

In the quiet of those late nights, I would creep into my girls' bedroom and watch them sleep. I enjoyed the serenity of their faces as they lay peacefully against the pillow. I relished the quiet intimacy of the maternal world. I would creep ever so slowly into their bedroom and lean in near their faces to make sure they were still breathing. It was the same gesture I'd made so many times when my daughter had been a baby in the crib. In the early days of her childhood, I would smooth the hair across her forehead and place a kiss on her sleeping brow. I made this gesture in gratitude for her life and the privilege to serve as her mother.

As I watched my girls sleep, I was swept away to the comfort of my own childhood memories. I recalled watching my father conduct his nightly ritual of tucking all of his children into bed. He would kiss our foreheads, brush away the hair, and place a sign of the cross upon our brows. My dad had explained that this ritual was a means of blessing his children and thanking God for his parenthood. On those first post-9/11 nights, I again felt the warmth of my father's touch. Even though he had been dead for seven years, I felt his gentle hand upon my brow. It tugged at my heart, stirring so many memories of how well Dad always protected his children. I longed to feel his touch and his comfort. I needed it so very much in these moments of turmoil. He had been my rock. He had been the anchor keeping me fastened to the earth. I had lost him all too soon. I understood the depth of the pain that comes with losing someone so precious. Perhaps my loss helped me better understand the pain of the victims' families, whom I would soon meet.

It is amazing to me how, as parents, we always see our children as the small babies we bore and rocked in our arms. It doesn't seem to matter how old, tall, or mature our children become. It doesn't matter that they are grown and now have children of their own. We always remember the simpler times, when they were children. Listening to the breathing of my loved ones satisfied some deep maternal instinct in me. It was a primal force, not easily explained. Each of those nights, the reality of the present situation would stir inside me. I wondered how many mothers were not ever again going to be able to kiss their children good night. How many of them still did not know the whereabouts of their loved ones? How long would it take to bring some resolution to all of the mothers who had suffered? I realized how very lucky I was. I had the ability to watch my family sleep. I relished those moments and thanked God for the gift to do so.

When I finally made it to bed, I found it difficult to sleep. I had never been a good sleeper. Even as a child, my mind never seemed to shut down and just rest. Now, in those twilight hours, I would reflect upon the vision of the angels in the field. In the safety of my home, I could ponder what I had seen. Each memory added more detail and emotion. My mind questioned, but my soul rejoiced in the possibility of what I had seen—and what was yet to be revealed. I had been a witness of God's benevolence. In some way, at some point in the future, I knew I would bear witness. I would give testimony of His gift to us that day.

Each morning, I awoke in a fog. I had barely fallen asleep when it was time to get moving again. Despite my fatigue, I was grateful to know I would soon be back at the site, where the demands of the day would once again require me to focus on my work. My duties left little time for anything but the task at hand. Great or small, these tasks allowed me to lose myself in a way that brought me comfort. Ever since my childhood, when I needed to de-stress I would clean the house. In some obscure way, the scrubbing of the floor or the polishing of the furniture provided me with a sense of relief. Delivering hot coffee, meeting with the other agency reps, or just talking with those most affected by the traumatic events helped relieve my tension in this stressful time.

But each morning as I left my beloved girls behind, I observed their anxiety. And I felt it in the very depth of my soul as well.

THE UNITED
AIRLINES TEAM

On the third day at the crash site, I was called to meet with a Pittsburgh Field Office administrator. He informed me that an issue had arisen between the law enforcement entities and the United Airlines (UA) team. The issue was causing conflict, and an immediate resolution was needed. I was asked to travel immediately to Seven Springs Mountain Resort and attempt to mediate the matter. The breach with UA was so urgent that I was to be flown by helicopter from the crash site to Seven Springs. The Seven Springs Resort, approximately 30 miles by car, had become the designated site for the coordination of all humanitarian efforts. It was where the United Airlines officials were headquartered, along with government agency officials, medical examiners, social service providers, and surviving family members of the Flight 93 passengers and crew.

A few minutes later, I arrived at the helicopter's makeshift landing pad, a little apprehensive at the prospect of flying in a helicopter. I'd flown in a small craft only once before, some 20 years earlier. I'd gone with a group of skydiver friends to watch them jump from the plane. It was a once-in-a-lifetime event—meaning I never took my friends up on the offer again! It was an experience I did not need to repeat. Moreover, after viewing the remains of Flight 93 just a few days previously, I did not relish the thought of flying, period. The initial images of the crash were forever etched into my mind.

I stepped into the craft apprehensively. The pilot greeted me and explained the flight plan and route we would take. He provided some safety tips and warned me to be very careful not to stare at the ground during the flight. Staring at the ground, he explained, might cause me to experience vertigo, so I should focus on the horizon instead. Before I knew it, we were hovering above the ground and heading to the resort.

When I arrived at Seven Springs a few minutes later, I was led to a large room in the lower level of the main lodge. I had visited the resort occasionally over the years, so the room was somewhat familiar. In the past, I'd been there for joyous occasions. The space was usually filled with people, food, vendors, and laughter. But today the room was quiet, having been transformed into a makeshift command center. Above the many rows of tables and telephones loomed signs bearing the names of various agencies. United Airlines, the National Transportation Safety Board (NTSB), and the Red Cross each had its designated area.

Off in the back left corner I noticed a group of about 15 people sitting around a large conference table. I was told this group was the UA contingency. As I approached the group, I was stopped by a tall man who presented a badge identifying him as the security chief for UA. He requested to know what business I had at Seven Springs. Providing him with my FBI credentials, I explained that I had been sent to mediate between UA and the law enforcement agencies. He nodded and escorted me to the table, where I was introduced to a woman who was identified as the group leader. Each of the UA staff then took turns introducing themselves and providing their job titles and duties. Although the group was very cordial in demeanor, I somehow felt as if I were being interrogated.

I spent about 90 minutes with the UA employees discussing the issues. As it turned out, the primary problem UA had with the law enforcement agencies concerned media coverage. It appeared that the law enforcement agencies were insistent that UA representatives provide information during routine press briefings. The UA administrators told me they were not at the crash site to provide information to the media. Rather, their primary purpose was to respond and assist with the humanitarian efforts. They were there to serve in the best interest of the Flight 93 crew members, the victims, and all their surviving family members. One of the group members reminded me that UA had also suffered substantial loss of human life. The airline had not only lost passengers but also crew members who were friends and colleagues.

As we delved into our discussion about media coverage, it seemed to me that there was a deeper problem we were not addressing. My intuition told me that the underlying issue was a breakdown in communication. Although the UA team members and the representatives from the law enforcement agencies were focused on the same thing—the crash site—neither side was aware of the others' purpose and desired outcomes. Each seemed to be confused by the meaning of the words spoken by the other. Each entity was addressing the issue in a different manner, creating a stalemate of sorts. The UA team was busy addressing the humanitarian effort, while the law enforcement personnel were focused on recovering evidence for the investigation. In the middle of all of this confusion were the family members of the victims of Flight 93.

After listening carefully to the concerns of the UA team, I recognized the problem was a breakdown in language. I had witnessed this language barrier too many times throughout my years in law enforcement. There seemed to be a missing link that often set a layperson into a defensive mode. The usual response from the law enforcement officer would be an offensive stance, which then caused a further rift between the two individual points of view. This language barrier was as evident to me now as it had been on my very first day of policing. I had been in the patrol car with my new partner, and we were driving to the station and making small talk. As we drove down a hill, we observed a young woman jogging. Without missing a beat in our conversation, he turned to me and said, "Nice body but no helmet."

I must have looked very perplexed, because he told me the woman's body was nice but her face was ugly. I was embarrassed—both by his statement and by my lack of knowledge of the lingo. I had grown up with five brothers, but it seemed I still had a great deal to learn about communicating with my fellow police officers!

As I continued my discussion with the UA team, the real issue became clear. The UA team was under impossible stress. They were saddened by the events of 9/11 and traumatized by their losses. To them, it appeared that their counterparts in law enforcement lacked the empathy and compassion needed to address the matter fully. They did not see that the law enforcement officers were also disheartened by the events, but in order for them to handle the circumstances, most had switched into their second personas—the "mechanism," as I mentioned earlier: "Just the facts, ma'am, just the facts." Such a "Joe Friday" demeanor appeared to the average person as indifference and a lack of real emotion.

In truth, even Detective Friday was using his defense mechanism to help him separate his emotions from the events. This mechanism is a necessary tool to separate heart and mind. As the left side of the brain works intensely on memorizing and analyzing all of the facts, the right side of the brain is crying out with emotion. It is a fragile tightrope, sometimes impossible to walk. At times, the thread connecting the two sides of the brain is frayed almost to the point of severing. Knowing this, I hoped I could provide some insight to the UA team to help them understand.

At the conclusion of our discussion, I rose from the table and shook hands. As I walked toward the door, I stopped in front of an older gentleman sitting in the corner of the room. I had noticed him upon my arrival and had been aware of his presence throughout the discussion. On occasion, I had noticed a UA team member glance in his direction. At several key moments in the conversation, the glances toward this man seemed to last longer. I extended my hand to the gentlemen and asked him if we had an agreement. He seemed perplexed.

"It's very apparent to me that you're in charge of this group," I said. He smiled, and his face relaxed.

"I guess you really are from the FBI," he said. "I feared you might be a media rep trying to mislead us as a means of obtaining some information."

"If I were the media," I said, laughing, "I'd hope I'd be much better dressed than these dirty fatigues! I have been driving an ATV for days, swallowing bugs at every turn. I wasn't even given any time to comb my hair or brush my teeth before I was flown here to meet with all of you."

"It's nice to see that members of the FBI have a sense of humor and haven't forgotten how to be human," he said.

I realized my hunch about the situation was right. I felt relieved to know there was indeed some hope to reduce the tension between us all. I again requested for him to confirm for me that I could report back to my supervisors that the conflict between the two entities had been resolved. He indicated I could tell my supervisors that all was well, but he added one stipulation. He requested that I be assigned to serve as the primary liaison to the UA administrative team. He also requested for me to be housed on site at Seven Springs with the other UA personnel and the surviving family members. He indicated this was a necessary step to improve the relationship with the UA team, who felt they needed a permanent liaison with the law enforcement agencies. Before I left the room, I shook hands with the gentleman—who by now had identified himself as the senior vice president in charge of the humanitarian response team representing UA.

From that first meeting, I knew I liked him. Despite the situation, he displayed a warm and welcoming smile and a calming demeanor. He exuded a confidence, which made me feel that everything would be all right. For a moment, the image of my deceased dad entered my mind, and it instantly made me feel safer. To this day, I am honored to consider this wonderful man my friend. In the years since, I have been privileged to remain in contact with him and other members of the UA team.

I left the building and was soon en route back to the crash site via helicopter. Upon my arrival I updated the field office administrator, relating the request for me to be housed at Seven Springs. Management agreed with the terms but indicated that I needed to make myself available at both sites. I queried how it would be possible to travel back and forth on a constant basis. I was told to speak with the Pennsylvania State Police site commander to determine if a trooper could be assigned to assist me. The PSP site commander agreed to provide two troopers to transport me between the two sites and to secure any services to accommodate the UA team. It appeared that my situation had changed once again.

A MOTHER'S AGONY

On Friday, September 14, the United Airlines team told me about the pending arrival of a Japanese family who had lost their only son on Flight 93. At the time of his death, the young man had been only 19 years old. I was advised that the family was en route from Japan and was due to arrive at Pittsburgh International Airport sometime on the 16th. The family would then travel to the Seven Springs site via limousine.

When the Japanese family members arrived at a private condominium in the mountains of Seven Springs, the law enforcement contingency immediately met with them. Also in attendance were Japanese diplomats, several interpreters, and representatives from United Airlines, the

National Transportation Safety Board, and the Red Cross. Once the introductions were complete, the interpreters began to convey the family's concerns. The parents were eager to know if their son had survived. Had he, or any of the passengers, used a parachute to escape from the plane? If their son had indeed perished, they requested the release of their son's remains. The interpreter told us that the family practiced Buddhism, and their religion required the imme-diate burial of the deceased.

On hearing the word *remains,* the law enforcement agency representatives indicated there was no body to bury. The translator was advised that the recovery efforts would take time, if there were any remains to be found at all. The man then passed this information on to the family.

The mother's demeanor instantly changed. I watched her carefully as her facial features became distorted. She rose from her chair and began to scream. The tears poured from her eyes. The extent of her agony was apparent to all. It could be heard in the tone of her voice and the pitch of the scream; it could be seen in her body language. She was distraught not only about losing her son but also about having no body to bury. There were no remains to place in the earth to which she could pay homage. She could not touch the face of her child one last time or whisper a final good-bye. Her little boy was gone, and there would be no final send-off, no ritualized ceremony to provide a blessing as his soul left its earthly domain.

I asked the interpreter if it was an appropriate gesture in Asian culture to console the grieving mother. I did not wish to add another insult to her already damaged heart. The translator indicated it was permissible to show emotion and concern. I stood up from the chair and reached for her. She fell into my arms and sobbed. We walked onto the outside patio and wept. As her tears merged with mine, I realized that no common language was necessary. Even though we did not speak the same tongue, we each instantly knew the other's heart. We shared a patois understood by all mothers. It is the language of love—the dance of life between a mother and her child. Her maternal heart synchronized with mine.

The heartbeat of a wounded parent who had just lost a beloved child was all too familiar to me. I had witnessed this behavior in both my personal and professional lives. I had lost close family members at an early age. And, as a police officer, it had been one of my duties to inform grieving family members that a child had been lost. One incident sprang immediately to mind—the death of an infant I'd witnessed many years before. He was only nine months old and had died from sudden infant death syndrome (SIDS). My partner and I received an emergency call concerning a baby who was not breathing. When we arrived at the home, the mother had met us at the door, frantically yelling, "Save my baby!"

She explained that her child was not breathing. As I tried to soothe her, my partner went to look at the baby. He peered into the crib and called me over. I walked over and saw a lovely little boy lying motionless in his bed. I noticed small traces of blood coming from his nose and ears, a sign of SIDS. I touched the child's lifeless body, and it was cold. I turned to the mother, but she just fell on her knees to the floor. I knelt down next to her as my partner called for the coroner. I will recall to my dying day the image of this mother kneeling on the floor and crying over the loss of her child. Her heart was broken, and her soul cried out to God for His mercy.

So many years later, I was once again relaying the news of one of life's tragedies. This wonderful young man's life had ended, along with the promise of what might have been. He was his family's hope for a prosperous future. This woman—this mother—had lost her only son, the son who was her true treasure in life, the greatest of her gifts. She had carried him in her womb and held him to her breast as he inhaled his first breaths. The world had dealt her such a cruel blow. Not only had her son died, but she would not be permitted to hold him one last time as he took his last breaths on earth.

To this day, my mind still travels back to a distant place and time when the rhythm of my heart was shattered, tainted by a mother's grief. Her primal scream rocked me to my very soul. She had been dealt the ultimate betrayal in life: she had outlived her child. She was another of the victims of Flight 93. The memory of her still floods the corners of my mind. Periodically, I wonder about her well-being and that of the rest of her family. Have they found peace? My hope is that this family will find some resolution, hearing my story of the angelic presence on that day. Even though we do not share a common language or religion, I am hopeful we share a spiritual understanding. It is an understanding and awareness that God does exist—a God who bears different names between us but the same universal concept. For in the worst moment of this mother's life, I know that God did intervene. I saw with my own eyes how God reached out and cared for her son when she could not, how He extended His hand and brought her little boy home.

CHAPTER

7

THE DAYS AT
SEVEN SPRINGS

For the next eight days, I moved around in a mind-
set of oblivion. I attended meeting after meeting, helping
arrange for the needs of the victims' families and easing
any problems that arose. Approximately 1,200 representatives from varying agencies spent many hours recovering
evidence, securing crime scene perimeters, interfacing with
government agencies and airline administrators, arranging
for additional resources, and assisting in coordinating the
two planned memorial services. Every one of us was engaged in a frenzy of activity; at times, the scene looked like
a staged event from some cop show. It was one of those
rare times when the reality of the job seemed to simulate the action of a television show, and we were all busily

working the scene. We were the consummate professionals performing our "call to service."

The site was our crime scene, and it had to be secured before we could dive into our tasks. Once the perimeters were set and the troopers were stationed to guard the property from unwanted trespassers, access was granted only to the necessary personnel. Within a short time, all on site were working in tandem and with reverence. Many I spoke with mentioned feeling like we were walking on hallowed ground, under the watchful eye of a higher power. Each time they shared their thoughts, I felt the urge to share my vision of the angels, but I did not.

From the outside, it may have appeared to the observer that chaos reigned at the site. But to the trained eye, each and every one of us was working with a purpose to complete our tasks. The dominoes were all falling into place. After the preliminary evidence was recovered, personnel began to move out across the neighborhood to identify possible witnesses and additional evidence. We waited with bated breath for answers that would help paint the entire picture and possibly help us draw some firm conclusions.

All of us worked extended shifts, willing to do what was required to resolve the unanswered questions of what happened on the plane. Were the passengers heroes— had they thwarted the hijackers' attempts? Would we find remains for each of the crew members and passengers on board? How many of the passengers and crew had left voice-mail messages for their loved ones? Did those messages contain information that would aid in the investigation?

Like everyone else, I barely had time to think as I moved through the motions to accomplish all the tasks at hand. I had little time to sleep, let alone ponder the vision of the angels. My energy was drained. It seemed that I had used up all of the magic God's angels had provided. I only looked forward to my return home and the comfort of my family. Then, and only then, might I have the opportunity to sort out the mystery of that moment on the field.

On my third night of sleeping at Seven Springs, I received a call from my daughter. She sounded very distressed about some problem with my granddaughter. My granddaughter was experiencing difficulty sleeping and had begun to regress in her daily habits. When my daughter would attempt to leave the little one at school, she would cry and panic. She was waking up in the middle of the night with nightmares, screaming out for me. When my daughter tried to talk to my granddaughter about the situation, she explained that she had overheard some older children talking about the events of 9/11. They had spoken of Afghanistan, terrorists, bombings, fighting, and thousands of dead people lying in the streets. Being only five years old and a kindergartner, my granddaughter had become anxious after hearing such talk. After hearing all of the chatter at school, she was worried that I was stationed in Afghanistan. She envisioned me in the middle of some hideous battle, with bodies covered in blood scattered around me and bombs blasting in every direction. She feared for her grandmother's safety and demanded my immediate return to her and our home.

My daughter was not sure how to explain the last few days to her child. After all, she had made a special effort to conceal the facts, to shield her daughter from any unnecessary worry. It was her job as a mother to protect her daughter from harm, so she'd stayed away from network

television and had replayed Disney videos and other cheer-
ful movies instead. She did this not only for her daughter
but also for herself. Each day at the U.S. Attorney's Office
had become harder than the one before. Her office was
in chaos, and the world was filled with pain and sorrow.
She had spoken to so many people, each of them expressing disbelief and fear. My daughter longed for the sanity
of our home. Our home was her only sanctuary. It was the
last retreat. It was a place where she could safely hold the
daughter whom she loved so dearly.

I took time to speak to my granddaughter. I reassured
her that I was safe and secure. I let her know I was not in
Afghanistan, nor in the middle of a battle. I explained that
there were no bodies lying around me and there were no
bombs. I was at Seven Springs Resort, I told her, reminding her that she had visited the resort with her mom and
me on Mother's Day and for Oktoberfest celebrations. She
listened carefully, and the tone of her voice seemed to calm
down. When I was finished speaking, she quietly requested,
"Swear to God you are okay."

"My right hand up to God," I responded.

My words seemed to relieve her worry. I assured her
I would call her every night and would be home in a
few more days. I requested that she be kind and caring
to her mother and that she help take care of the family dog. I let her know of my love for her and her mom.
Then I whispered good night and hung up the phone. In
the quiet minutes following that call, I prayed for God's
help and wisdom to carry on. My heart and soul cried in
silence for the warmth and comfort of my granddaughter's sweet little arms. I longed to just hold her and make
her pain go away. Or was it my own pain I was longing
to have soothed?

The first Saturday following the events of 9/11, I asked for a few hours' leave. I had so wanted to see the girls and provide some comfort to them. I wanted to hug and hold them for my sake, as well. I had also arranged to have my brother bring a friend's backhoe to our house, to dig a hole in the corner of my backyard. The plan for the hole was to build a pond where I would place a statue of the Blessed Mother. In the days following the angel sighting, I longed for a little grotto in which I could meditate and pray. I realize now that I wanted a reminder of the angels, somewhere I could give homage for the gifts received. In the deepest part of my soul lies a commitment to my religious beliefs and upbringing. It beckoned to me to erect a symbol of my belief in the Creator, to give Him thanks for the gifts He had bestowed upon me. As I had such a meaningful relationship with the Mother Mary, I thought it befitting to have Her statue nearby.

For a few months following 9/11, I moved through the process of digging the pond's foundation and placing the stones in the form of a tiny mounted grotto. On the day Mary was placed at the top of a circular stone, I was elated to know the job was finally complete. In the intervening years I have found great comfort in her presence in my backyard. From each of the rear windows of my home, I can look out and see the lovely white cement statue with the delicate facial features, the signature of Mary's grace and elegance.

On many occasions I walk to that corner of the yard and say a prayer. Each time, I feel the warmth and comfort of the Blessed Mother's presence. When I am near the statue, I shut my eyes and I can feel Her touching me, consoling my fears and anxieties. As She wraps Her white light of grace and blue robe of protection around me, I feel my energy shift in a positive direction and my spirit come to life. To this day, my beloved Mother and friend stands in the corner of my backyard, ever watchful, surrounded by plants, trees, and soft-hued flowers. There are days when many birds gather around the statue. On occasion a brilliant male cardinal perches on the tree above. As the red bird sings a beautiful aria to the sky, I feel joy ring through my heart and in my soul.

THE MEMORIAL SERVICES

During the second week at the crash site, two memorial services were held. The first was scheduled for Tuesday and the second was on Thursday. Those of us working at the crash site and Seven Springs were tasked to complete the preparations for the services. We had been advised that there would be many dignitaries in attendance, including Mrs. Bush and Mrs. Cheney. The days prior to the memorial services were filled with innumerable meetings to arrange for all the details. We spent time developing an agenda and handouts for the occasion. There was a great deal of work to accomplish to address the needs of the family members at Seven Springs and to recover the human remains at the crash site.

On Tuesday, I was asked to ride in the lead vehicle leading the buses of the victims' family members from Seven Springs to the crash site. As we traveled through the small town of Shanksville, the residents of the community lined the streets with American flags and waved them with such pride. There were banners containing words of sympathy, kindness, and well wishes for those seated on the buses. As I peered out the window, I tried to swallow the tears in my throat, but I was unsuccessful. The tears made their watery pathway down my face and I noticed I was not alone. The uniformed trooper seated in the car with me was crying, too. I watched as tears streamed from his eyes to his chin. He looked forward in an effort to avoid my eyes, not breaking his trancelike state. Even as he focused on his duties, I could see that this wonderful, strong man had been touched by the generous nature of the residents of this small community. In that moment, the trooper confirmed for me that it was all right to feel compassion and to cry.

Of all the days in my law enforcement career, this was my proudest moment. For as we traveled closer to the site, the Pennsylvania State Police troopers stood in full military salute in honor of the victims and their families. From the farthest security points away from the site, to the closest in proximity to the services, each trooper stood erect and on point. As we passed each uniformed officer, they seemed to display a paradox of emotion and demeanor. Despite their stance, I could see tears in their eyes. Not only were they there to secure the scene and protect those in attendance from any further danger, they were there to share their humanity. The image of these wonderful men and women still remains in my mind as the epitome of strength and character. They symbolized the American spirit and helped remind all who were present of the true meaning of honor.

When we arrived at the field, the troopers in their freshly pressed uniforms lined the path leading to the crash site and paved the way for the family members to walk to the memorial service. As the family members passed by the officers, each of them proudly saluted. It was an amazing sight to see. These wonderful men and women in their pressed gray uniforms, hats, and neatly polished shoes were there to comfort those suffering immense loss and pain.

During the service, one of the deceased victim's wives was trying to contain her small son. It was obvious that she was distraught with her son's behavior. Just as she began to lose her composure and cry, a lieutenant from the Pennsylvania State Police came to her aid. He took the small boy by the hand and led him to one of the mounted troopers. The lieutenant exchanged some words with the trooper, who immediately dismounted from the horse. The lieutenant then placed the small boy on the horse and gently guided him a short distance away from his mother and the crowd. Again, the humanity of the moment touched my heart, and I felt a wave of admiration.

These examples of kindness and compassion remind me why most law enforcement professionals I know answered their call to service in the first place. They did so in the best interest of their fellow humans.

Amid all the pomp and circumstance of the memorial services, several moments stand out in my mind. The most memorable moments did not come from the numerous politicians and bureaucrats delivering their speeches. They did not have to do with the diplomats who were required to be present because of their positions. They came from the support of the average citizens—the Girl Scouts who weaved red, white, and blue beads in the shape of the American flag, the schoolchildren drawing pictures and printing words on construction paper to remind us of their gratitude, the local residents waving banners and flags with such pride. I felt an extreme sense of patriotism as I watched the residents of Shanksville greet and escort the victims' family members as they traveled toward the crash site. They were there to share their hearts and compassion with the walking wounded who were seated on the buses. People stood on the curbs and sidewalks surrounding their homes as a tribute to the victims of Flight 93. I'm sure that the memories of their own family members stood at the forefront of their minds, as my thoughts turned to my own family and the longing to be near them as well.

Another outstanding memory that stays with me is that of Mrs. Bush. I recall thinking upon meeting her that she was such a First Lady. As she read her speech, it was clear that she, too, had been deeply affected by the events of 9/11. Yet despite her inner turmoil, she was poised, sympathetic, and sincere with the words she shared. At the conclusion of the formal ceremony, Mrs. Bush lingered. She stayed and talked with all who were present. She spent time with each of the family members who desired to speak with her. She even extended her hand to those of us who were working at the sites. Mrs. Bush took the time to shake our hands and thank us for our hard work in the name of the victims. By her presence and her natural ease with people, she, too, had served the greater good. All of us were very much in need of her comfort that day.

THE RETURN HOME

I remained at the site for 12 long and grueling days. On Saturday, September 23, I was finally going home to be with my family. I was elated at the prospect of laying my weary body on my own bed and spending quality time with my daughter and my granddaughter. I was hopeful that just seeing my family would help to balance my mind and soul.

As I opened the front door of my home, I was greeted by the smiling faces of my daughter and granddaughter. My little darling ran straight to me and laced her arms around my waist as she hugged me. We stood there for a minute, and I relished the moment of my homecoming. It felt great to hold my grandchild again—to hear her express her love for me. Since the time she could walk and talk, she had greeted me at the door every day, flinging her tiny arms around my legs and screaming, "Situ is home." I am Lebanese by heritage and *Situ* means grandmother in Arabic.

This was our ritual, and so it was on this day, too. But on this particular occasion, my eyes welled with tears at the sight of both my girls. The touch of those small hands permeated my skin and traveled to the very core of my heart and soul. I was so grateful to have the fortune of reuniting with my family, who had been safely nestled here amid so much tragedy.

As I knelt down and hugged my lovely little creature, my mind returned to the vision of the many grieving family members whom I had met at Seven Springs. Each of their faces had been scanned in the memory card of my mind. Each of their stories was forever etched in the tunnels of my ears. Each of their deceased family members had a place in my tattered soul.

The memory of the previous days remains within me like a finely detailed sketch. I can still recall my first glance at the field at Shanksville. Little did I know that the image would never leave me. In fact, it would grow more vivid with each passing year.

In the aftermath of the horrific events of 9/11, the crash site, the victims' family members with their individual stories of loss, the memorial services, and all of the stress, it was astounding to me that the robotic trance that had taken hold some two weeks before was instantly stilled by the touch of my granddaughter's tiny hands. I felt my heart melt at the sensation of her fingers pressing against my legs. In all of my years in law enforcement, I had wrestled with the transition between the two personalities contained inside of me. But that day, I realized all it took to change me from my superwoman persona was the simple touch of a loved one. It was then that I truly understood the power of love.

Later that evening, sitting on the couch in "my seat," I cherished us all being together. It had felt like a lifetime since we'd been able to interact as a family. How wonderful it was to be with them again. I relished their presence and enjoyed the warmth of our home. I smelled the familiar fragrances of the room. I saw the family photographs lined up neatly on the wall of the stairwell. I smiled at the familiar faces and touched a photo of my dad as a silent prayer. The glass and gold frames gleamed in the sun. How simple it all seemed. These were the thoughts that had sustained me through the previous weeks. I had all the important pleasures in my life. I had the love of my family and the blessings of my home. How many of us had taken all these things for granted prior to 9/11? My father had always called me a simpleton. It was a term I hadn't exactly appreciated, but what he meant was that I took delight in the smallest of things. In those initial days post 9/11, I took great pleasure in the simplest thing—my return to my girls and our tiny home set on the hill above the Allegheny River.

I was only home for a few hours when my granddaughter demanded to know more about the Seven Springs Resort. I reminded her once again that she had visited the resort with me on several occasions. Try as I might, however, I could not convince her that the spot had been a safe haven. She insisted that I was not being truthful with her. As she debated the issue with me, I realized that she, too, had been traumatized by the events of the past weeks. Even though she had been sheltered from all of the daily news releases, she had still been touched by what had transpired and what she had heard. She'd listened to the whispers of other children recounting stories from countless news stories. Regardless of their intentions, the adults around her had been incapable of shielding her from the hardships of 9/11.

I decided that there was only one way to resolve our standoff. I told my daughter to pack a bag for my granddaughter, because we would be traveling back to Seven Springs together. I explained that it was the only way for the little one to understand. She needed to see the resort for herself and walk the surrounding properties so she could be assured that I had been safe. It would be the only way for her to fully comprehend that the nightmares she'd been experiencing were images she had created based on limited information. I made a quick call to the front desk of the resort to arrange for a room, and we got into my car and traveled to Seven Springs.

On the drive up, I continually had to reassure my granddaughter that we would be safe and no harm would come to either of us. The ride seemed to take longer than it had over the previous two weeks. I realized that I was driving much slower than normal. I always seemed to slow down when the little one was in my car. But before too long, we arrived on the Seven Springs properties.

Although it was nighttime, the lights in the parking lot illuminated the areas around the resort and allowed us to see the many buildings and grounds. As we looked at our surroundings, my granddaughter became more peaceful. The once-taut muscles of her mouth and forehead relaxed and eased away the frown. She turned to me and smiled.

"So, this is where you stayed," she said.

"Yes, so this is where I stayed," I responded.

We entered the building and walked around without saying another word. Before too long, we met up with some of the United Airlines personnel who had not yet left the site. We sat for a while and talked with the others, but soon my granddaughter laid her head on my lap and fell asleep. My heavy heart filled with such warmth and emotion. I captured the moment in my memory and whispered my thanks to God. I was grateful for the reminder that I had a wonderful life. It was full of significance and family to love. It had a purpose; I was truly blessed. I lifted my granddaughter from my lap and carried her to our room. We spent a quiet and uneventful night at the resort sleeping. As the memories of 9/11 passed through my mind, I found some peace lying next to this child. She was the center of my life and my future legacy. As I listened to her quiet snoring, I fell asleep as well. It was the first real rest I had since that fateful morning of September 11.

CHAPTER

10

THE RECKONING BETWEEN MIND AND SPIRIT

It would take a full year—until the first anniversary of 9/11—for me to come to grips with the vision of the angels on the field. That day, a memorial service had been planned at the crash site in Shanksville. I intended to participate in the service and visit those with whom I had spent so much time in the days post-9/11. I would, of course, also be revisiting the site where I'd first seen the angelic vision.

I arrived in Shanksville with great apprehension and anxiety. I had not slept the night before, and my exhaustion was not helping my mood. As I walked through the crowd, I saw many familiar faces. Some attendees were victims' family members and some were representatives from United Airlines and the government. Their faces had pierced my mind many times in dreams over the course of the intervening year. I spent a few moments catching up, anxious to hear their news. Then I took a brief stroll to look at the site, attempting to retrace my steps of one year ago. But the grounds did not look the same. With all the people milling around, I became disoriented in my direction.

My attention was drawn to the memorial service, which had just begun. Despite the fact that it was a somber event and the weather was somewhat overcast, the service was elegant and beautifully staged. I listened, aware of the vibrations around me. I kept hoping for a second opportunity to see the angels. I made a silent prayer for God to give me a sign to validate what I had seen on my first visit to this site. It wasn't too long before my prayers were answered, and I received my sign. During the ceremony, as the voices lifted in a solemn song, a wind ripped through the field. It reverberated off the makeshift theater's metal roof, loud and hard. For a brief moment, all were silenced as the mighty wind echoed through the amphitheater. All at once, the music sounded and eased my mind of the memories of a burning plane. The wind blew and cleared the pain. The voices of the family members around me reminded me that I was not alone. I remembered again that we are never truly alone. As fast as the wind came in, it was gone. The wind had given me my answer. It was true: I really had been given a blessing. I had seen God's angels walking the earth on one of the worst days in American history. I had been honored and privileged to witness them. The only question left was, "Why me?"

Later that evening, in the still of the night and the quiet of my home, I reflected on the events of the previous year. I had wondered many times if I had lost my mind on 9/11. I had spent much of the year feeling isolated and alone. I knew I had to talk to someone—and very soon. As I questioned who it was I should talk to, my mind began to hear the words of a poem.

In troubled times of my life, I had often written poetry. I wrote down the words of this poem and put them away for safekeeping. I placed them in a book—a book I did not return to until August 2008. At that time I was sorting through my book collection, organizing the books onto shelves in the upstairs bedroom of my home, when I came across the poem. It reads as follows:

I said good-bye today
It didn't remove the pain
It didn't remove the memories
Not the good not the bad
The good-bye brought me no closure
I said good-bye today
To my past, to my present, and to my future
I let go of all my dreams
I let go of all of my wonder
I said good-bye today
While a distant trumpet played
While the sighs, the tears, and the words echoed
    across the sky
As I stood in silence searching for one face for one
    spirit to rise from the plain
I said good-bye today
In an open space of time
In a field sometimes forgotten and filled with
    unknown names
Not kindred to warmth
Not kindred to the rhythm of my soul

I said good-bye today . . .

The poem had some truth to it. I *had* said good-bye. But I had not eradicated the pain of that day. I merely buried it deep inside my heart, where it lay waiting for the time when I was ready to face it.

FIRST CONFESSION

A few days passed after the first anniversary event before I made the decision to talk to someone about my experiences on 9/11. Because of my Catholic upbringing, I needed to seek the counsel of a priest. I felt the desire to reach out and confess. I was in so much turmoil about 9/11 in particular but also about all the mistakes I had made throughout my life that had made me feel less than worthy. I had dwelled on the negative aspects for so long that I had no real ability to see the positive—or my path back to my inner beauty. I could not see myself for the kind and caring person I am. I wondered why I couldn't extend the same courtesy and compassion to myself that I had for others in my life. It seemed my strict upbringing had left me with little ability to forgive myself for any of my own trespasses. These feelings only compounded my anxiety and caused me to feel like an unworthy recipient of God's amazing grace.

In addition to these feelings, I wanted so much to share another secret with the priest—something I had long kept hidden. Since childhood, I had seen visions of Saint Michael the Archangel. On occasion, Michael would appear and whisper some words of wisdom or a cautionary warning in my right ear. Although I had firmly believed the Archangel was present in my life, I had rarely spoken of his existence. As a small child, when I would mention the angelic sightings to family members, I was reprimanded. They pushed away the vision as some imaginary childhood manifestation. Because of this, my hesitation in revealing the story of the angels at the crash site felt justified in my mind and validated in my heart.

As I grew into adulthood, the visions of Michael—and his whispers in my ear—continued. But as I advanced in age, I started to believe angelic visitations were granted only to a privileged few who had lived devout and chaste lives. For my part, I had learned about life through a series of hard lessons. I had lived and breathed through many mistakes. I pondered all the people whom I believed to be more worthy of angelic sightings than the likes of me. I did not feel that I had earned such a blessed gift. Because of these feelings, and a need to understand the purpose of the event, I decided it was now time to share my amazing story with another person.

I questioned who it should be. If I told someone at work, surely they would think I was suffering from a mental illness. If I told my family, they might worry I had succumbed to emotional stress. Instead, I decided to talk to a priest. I chose a man who had become a friend, spiritual counselor, and one of the few people who would be sworn to secrecy by his own vows of silence.

The next day, I called him. As soon as I heard his voice, I became emotional and found it almost impossible to speak. I regained some composure and requested a meeting to discuss a problem. When we met a few days later, I revealed to him my story of the angels. He listened very intently and thanked me for the privilege of sharing such a powerful event with him. I told him that I was deeply troubled by two questions. First, had my mind played tricks on me, or had I really seen a vision? Second, if I really had seen the angels, why me? I had not lived a perfect life. I was not devout like others I knew. I had made so many mistakes in my life.

My priest friend explained that God did not look at me as a sinner. God looked at me as one of His children. He had forgiven my wrongdoings, and He was telling me that it was time for me to forgive myself. He was giving me the grace to move forward and share this miraculous story. God wanted others to know that He was there on that fateful day. He sent His angels to recover His children who had lost their lives. I knew my friend was right, because I was filled with hope for a new beginning. It was time to move on with a life filled with new beginnings.

At the conclusion of our discussion, I realized the magnitude of his words. I realized that my status does not matter at all. I am not a queen, king, aristocrat, or president. I am not perfect. I am, like many others affected by 9/11, an imperfect child of God who has made many errors in my choices. But the only mistakes that matter are the ones we don't learn from. Oh, and I have learned.

I remember as a child my father reading to my siblings and me from the Bible. When I was seven or eight, he read the Ten Commandments out loud. At that age, it seemed like a lot of information to digest! When he had finished reading, I said to him, "Daddy, I'll never remember all of those rules."

"Lillie Marie," he responded, "there are many rules to remember. But if you live your life by the simple rule of never intentionally hurting another person, then you will be following God's commandments."

After listening to the priest's comments, I understood what Dad had meant. My mistakes did not matter. By serving as a law enforcement officer, I had made my atonement to God. It was obvious that God had forgiven me. Now, it was time for me to forgive myself.

Forgiveness is the true essence of life. It is a passage we must go through. It quakes the very core of our being. Forgiving ourselves is essential if we want to move forward on the path. I had been held hostage in the gathering of life's atrocities, which seemed to merge into one by my unwillingness to forgive myself. Memories and pain were festering deep inside me. It was not possible to move forward with my life if I could not first let go of the past.

Remembering the words of my beloved dad, I was able to recapture my heart's contentment. Forgiveness had provided a spiritual renewal. It had allowed my soul to soar to new heights. It had expanded my mind in ways I would never have imagined. The forgiveness I attained had helped the malady to heal. The malignancy of self-loathing that had weighed me down for so many years had drifted into the oblivion. Oh yes, the forgiveness came in the recall of not just the past deeds, but for time served in the protection of others.

A REFLECTION OF MARY MAGDALENE

The impact of my discussion with the priest took a few days to truly sink in. On one particular evening, I was collecting my thoughts and analyzing them. As I worked through some facts, my thoughts drifted to a book my dad had given to me years before—*Jesus the Son of Man* by the Lebanese prophet Kahlil Gibran. The book provides interpretations of Jesus' first meetings with some of the most significant people in his life. One of the passages in particular had caught my eye—Jesus' first encounter with Mary Magdalene. That story felt so relevant in this moment of self-forgiveness. After all, Mary Magdalene had changed her life completely upon her first encounter with Jesus. Because Jesus had seen her true essence, the beauty that dwelled in her soul, he had forgiven her. His love for Mary Magdalene gave her permission to love herself. In that instant of recognition by Jesus, her heart opened and she changed her own image to reflect Jesus' light.

All my life I had a special relationship with the two Marys of the Bible—Mary the Mother of God and Mary Magdalene. I had prayed to Mary our Mother of Perpetual Help since the birth of my daughter. On the morning following her birth, my mom gave me my first prayer book honoring the Mother. From that moment on, I dedicated my heart to Mary and prayed to our lady on a daily basis. Since I built the grotto in my backyard, I've knelt in prayer to her every single day. Each day I bend down to bid her a good morning and a good night. As I open the blinds, I say to her statue, "Good morning, my beloved mother and friend."

These two Marys, each with her unique lifestyle, shared the love of a man. One shared Jesus' life as his mother and the other shared it as his devoted colleague and friend. One of them was pure and chaste and the other was free-spirited and worldly. As a woman, I reflect the traits of both. My inner soul reflects the purity of Mary's love for her son. Both of us welcomed a child into our lives at a young age. We share the knowledge of motherhood and its bond to the universal energy.

My humanity also reflects the imperfection of a woman. I was and still am a woman who has made mistakes in her life. Like Mary Magdalene, I, too, have experienced pain. I have reveled in the shadow of the admiration of men. I have made choices of which I am ashamed, choices that did not inspire me to become a better person. Yet post-9/11, I have chosen a new path—a path of self-forgiveness and enlightenment.

That day on the field, God gave me the gift of His divine grace. He had peered inside my being, into the recesses of my heart and soul, and had found its sheer purity. He had located my inner perpetual light, just as He did with Mary Magdalene. This lovely pure light sustained itself in spite of difficulties and temptations. It was acknowledging my own purity of heart that allowed me to finally accept His gift.

Our beliefs matter the most. If we accept our own inner strength, we can take the right action on behalf of ourselves and others. Our beliefs teach us to trust, and this trust guides our path. Mine has been a long and arduous journey, but one I would gladly embrace again. For in this odyssey of discovery and retribution, I have made an important discovery: I've come to know God is here. He is here in the essence of the warm morning sun as it gazes down upon His earth. He is here in the faces of His people as they turn to look toward Heaven. He is here in the laughter of His children as they dance and sing His praises. He is here in His kindness and grace. His grace was here on that fateful day of 9/11. God extended His hand to His children, and I was privileged to witness His "field of angels" and bear testimony of His benevolence.

A TRAUMATIC INJURY

In June 2005 I began to experience some severe health issues. I spent months visiting doctors trying to find out what was wrong. My primary care physician noted a decline in my health since my involvement at the Flight 93 crash site. She believed that I had been traumatized in some way and that my autoimmune system had been compromised. She recommended that I see several specialists to investigate further.

By that time I was beginning to see a clear pattern in my symptoms. Any stress, no matter how mild, caused me to experience high anxiety. Then, a painful migraine would take hold, starting in the mid-point area at the back of my head. Soon my entire body would stiffen from the pain. It often felt like someone had placed a steel girdle inside my body and kept pulling it tighter and tighter until I was unable to breathe. The whole time I could feel the rapid firing of my adrenaline repeatedly sending the signals of fight or flight to my brain. When the chest pains started, I felt my first glimpse of the fear of death. Then came the anxiety attacks with the profuse sweating, hyperventilating, and adrenaline rushes. It was during these times that I felt the most vulnerable.

What finally drove me to see the doctors was my daughter. She kept pointing out changes in my behavior, how I had become overly anxious about the simplest of situations. She kept telling me that I was overreacting to minor events in our lives. As a result of her continued concern, I scheduled appointments with the specialists my doctor had recommended. When I look back at this period in my life, I am grateful for the grace that was bestowed upon me, because without it I'm not sure I would have survived to share this story of God's love.

After a few months, many doctors' visits, and a series of diagnostic tests, I was told I was suffering from post-traumatic stress disorder (PTSD). The testing had ruled out any other major contributing factors. Stress, the doctors told me, was responsible for all my health difficulties. I had an extremely hard time accepting this diagnosis. After all, I had always been a superwoman. I was strong and invincible, capable of handling any problem. I had accomplished a great deal in my life and weathered many a storm. I didn't have time for PTSD.

But the more I reflected on it and the more I learned about the disorder, the more plausible it seemed. It was true—I was holding a lot inside. I hadn't allowed myself to feel as most women did. I had hidden my feminine essence as a means of self-protection on the job. I could not get emotionally involved with victims, nor was I permitted any emotional displays. I was trained to tamp down all of my thoughts and feelings so I could serve and protect.

This need to suppress my true feelings came as a result of my role as a "spectator" in my new world of the "testosterone jungle." I had placed the special part of my femininity in a secret hiding place. The more deeply I buried the female in me, the more I forgot who I was. I took on a new identity, starting one memorable night early in my law enforcement career.

On a quiet Sunday evening, in my first few months on the job, I was dispatched to respond to a vehicle accident with injuries. The dispatcher indicated that the accident had taken place outside a local church that was located in the neighboring community. The church in question just happened to be the one my family had attended for several generations. As I arrived at the accident scene, I saw that a vehicle had struck a very large tree that was located in a lot adjacent to the church. The vehicle was badly damaged. As I approached the car, I saw that there was an elderly woman lying on the street. She was barely moving, and it was obvious that she was gravely injured. I rushed to her and discovered that her breathing was very labored and raspy.

As I lifted her into my arms, I noticed there was another woman still seated inside the car. I could see only the top of her torso; the front end of the car had collapsed around the poor woman. As I looked closer at the two injured women, I realized that I knew them. They were elderly sisters who were fellow parishioners and who always sat in the front pews at Sunday mass. Throughout my years as a child I admired their lovely ladylike attire, complete with hat and gloves.

Back at the scene, emergency personnel were now responding. Several police officers had arrived, as had the firefighters and the emergency medical personnel. As the firemen extricated the second woman from the car, I turned my attention toward the woman in my arms. Her breathing was becoming more labored. I noticed that she was bleeding from several locations, and there were bones protruding from parts of her arms and legs. I held her in my arms and prayed for her well-being. Soon she became unconscious, and I was grateful for her reprieve from the pain. In a few minutes, the parish priest arrived and began to administer last rites. As the priest anointed her with oil, my heart was moved by the ritual. I found it hard to stay detached from all that was taking place. I had never before observed such an anointing, and I was overcome by emotion knowing that a human being was dying in my arms.

It was then that I noticed the many spectators who were watching the events. My heart cried out for the poor woman to be given some privacy. I could not fathom why anyone would want to stand around watching another person suffer in such a manner. I tried to keep control of my emotions, but I felt my eyes fill with tears. In that moment, the grief became too much and I began to cry. As the tears streamed down my face, I heard one of the firemen say, "You see? This is why we don't want women working as police officers. A woman can't do the job. Men don't cry while they are working and women do."

No sooner had the fireman finished his comments than I heard one of my fellow police officers respond. "She is doing her job, and at the same time showing compassion for someone who is obviously dying. Be quiet and let her alone. She is a good officer, and I'm proud to work with her."

Without another word, the responders turned back to their work. Soon, the woman lying in my arms succumbed to her injuries. As she stopped breathing, I realized that I had held someone in my arms as they had died. My tears flowed in a steady stream, and my heart ached for the life that had now ended. The medical personnel took her from my arms and lifted her onto a gurney. Within a few minutes she was covered with a white blanket and placed inside the ambulance.

At that moment, I realized the gravity of the work I was involved in. It was going to be more than just responding to routine calls. There would be times when someone's life would lie precariously in my hands. I wondered if the male firefighter had been right. Was my gender a hindrance on the job?

This accident was one of the first tragedies I ever witnessed up close. It was also my initial exposure to gender discrimination on the force, men who questioned my ability to work as a police officer while responding to a call for service. In retrospect, I occasionally think of the officer who rushed to defend me. He provided strong words of wisdom not only to the firefighter but to me as well. He gave me the approval I needed not only as a woman but as a rookie cop. Although he had reassured me that it was all right to be myself as a police officer, inside I knew it would be the last time I would cry at the scene. My ego would not allow it, especially not in front of the men. And my ego did not soften its stance over time. To the contrary, it grew stronger with each passing year. It became an ingrained part of me, with a life force of its own. And now it was deeply affecting my ability to reason as I faced my diagnosis of PTSD.

In fact, I ignored the diagnosis for more than two years. In the meantime, my life was in a lot of turmoil. The anxiety had gotten so bad that it was nearly impossible to hide it on the job. Then, in the fall of 2007, my world as I knew it came crashing down around me. It happened while I was cleaning my office inside the FBI complex. Unable to hide my symptoms any longer, I considered resigning my position and leaving the Bureau.

As I was cleaning out my desk, I came across a notebook. At a glance I knew exactly what it was: my original notes about Flight 93. I decided not to open it there but instead to take it home with me. It was a Friday afternoon, and I decided I'd read it over the weekend. When I got home that night I eagerly opened the notebook and began to read through it. To my surprise, I was immediately transferred to the crash site. It was as if no time had passed. I was there on the field, surrounded by the trees. I saw the hole where the plane had sunk into the earth. I saw the ponds filled with water and debris. I saw the firefighters with their tarnished and emotionless faces.

I began to feel highly agitated and claustrophobic. A kaleidoscope of emotions arose in succession, culminating in sobs. I heard myself wail and yell with anger. It took me a few minutes to realize that I wasn't at the crash site, but sitting in my bed. I then became so ill that I was in bed for two days.

A few days following this episode, I had an appointment with my primary care physician. I apologized for my initial inability to accept her diagnosis and explained about reading the notes and the resulting health crisis. I told her I realized my resistance to the PTSD was just my ego. Up to that point in my life, I hadn't understood just how huge my ego was. In some ways it had ruled me. It had found a home in my stubbornness and called itself strength. It had dug itself deeply into the trenches of my mind and would not give any ground. My doctor laughed at me, but then her eyes welled up with tears.

"Your best personality traits are also your worst," she said.

I laughed at her words and said, "Ever since I was a child, I have always been told that I'm my own worst enemy."

How true I understood these words to be. I had a tough time trusting myself—and others, too. As a child, so many years earlier, my trust had been destroyed. I had been sexually abused by a trusted adult. He not only robbed me of my innocence but also tortured my heart, my mind, my body, and my soul. What he had robbed from me all those years ago had taken great effort to regain. The many years of life that followed the abuse only added to my pain and sorrow. It had left me with self-doubt and a lack of trust for others. While I attempted to reach out repeatedly, each time I would retreat to a safe haven. There in my domain, I would guard the internal structure of my heart. It's why I had become Superwoman, after all. As Superwoman, I didn't need to rely on anyone else's help. I was invincible and self-sustaining. I could defeat any foe and rid myself of any problem.

Boy, did I need a reality check—and it had arrived. It announced itself in the form of illness. My body now reflected the ravaging of my soul.

CHAPTER

14

THE FLASHBACKS: A RETURN TO THE SCENE

A few days following the incident with the notebook, I experienced another flashback. I was at the gas station and was standing near a man who was putting diesel fuel into his pickup truck. I inhaled some of the fumes and was again mentally transferred to the crash site. I was in the mobile command unit, arriving at the scene. The firemen with their equipment were just leaving the site. The burning smells of fuel and pine entered my nose. The world stood still for a few moments and I remembered the field. It was as if time had stood still and it was 9/11 all over again. It took me a few moments to regain my composure.

This flashback was the last straw. I had no choice but to finally accept the diagnosis of PTSD. A few weeks later I had another visit with my primary care physician. She was elated, feeling that my acceptance of PTSD would be a turning point in my healing process. She explained that mental trauma was like alcoholism. As long as I denied my condition, she could not treat it appropriately.

A few days later, on the day of my third granddaughter's baptism, I experienced another flashback. This one was even more worrisome than the previous ones. It happened as the priest was giving a sermon on the significance of baptism, talking about the crucifixion of Jesus. According to the Bible, he told us, the earth quaked and the ground opened up as Jesus died on the cross. When the earth opened, the Saints rose up from the ground in reverence to the Son of God and His extreme sacrifice to humankind.

As the priest uttered these words, my mind again traveled to the crash site—and the field of angels standing and waiting. I viewed them in all of their revelry and splendor. They stood tall, strong, and vigilant. Again, as if I were at the crash site, I felt all of the emotional sensations of 9/11. I became extremely disoriented and did not know where I was. I felt the others around me in the pews, but the crash site was there, too. I panicked. It took me three or four minutes to come back to where I was, standing in the church with my family members around me. How real the flashback had felt. It had all the same sights and smells, all of the confusion. But, interestingly, this time there were no other people there. I was at the scene all alone. I stood in the middle of the field and felt myself swirling. I looked across the pond and saw my angels standing there. They were there, just as they had been on 9/11. I began to cry. I was somehow cognizant of the tears running down my face. At that moment my eldest granddaughter took notice and placed her hand on my arm. Her touch brought me back to the present time, just as her touch had brought me back to reality post-9/11. It was extremely difficult to focus, but I smiled at her and attempted to regain my composure.

"Are you all right?" she inquired.

"My tears were those of joy and not of pain," I lied. My dearly loved granddaughter smiled and snuggled in toward me in the pew.

The rest of that Sunday moved in oblivion. This of all days should have been one of complete joy. I had once again been blessed with a new granddaughter. It was supposed to be a day of celebration, yet my being lacked the ability to feel joy. I tried to compose myself and appear as if all was well. But as the day passed, I could feel tremors inside my body. I knew it was going to be a rough day and an even tougher night.

All night I lay in bed trying to sleep. My body was restless, and my mind had no reprieve from constant thoughts. I had no peace from the tremors inside my body. The tremors always scared me. They were unsettling and always heightened my fear. I had no control of my body; it would not respond to my will. I longed for words of comfort from my father. I needed him so desperately. I needed him to tell me that all would be well soon. I longed to scream aloud and tell everyone of my hurt. If only the pain were apparent from the outside so the world could see the magnitude of my wounds. It would be obvious to all that I had been deeply wounded by my experience at the crash site. But I had been rendered silent—both by the enormity of the destruction and by my inability to tell the world about the angels in the field.

CHAPTER

15

A SPIRITUAL SURRENDER

The day following the flashback in church I again became very ill. I was in a state of high anxiety and hypervigilance and lost focus regarding my day-to-day tasks. I was so upset by the flashback that I contacted my physician for counsel. I also spoke to my priest. I spent the next five days trying to revive my body and my mind.

One week later I finally understood the message God was sending me. The flashback had been symbolic in nature. The passengers and crew members of Flight 93 sacrificed their lives, just as Jesus had sacrificed himself for the benefit of humankind. In those first frightening moments on the plane, the passengers and crew didn't know the details of the hijackers' plans. They weren't aware of their intended destination. However, they did know of the three prior acts of terrorism. Through all of the telephone calls the passengers had made and received while on board the plane, they knew about the fate of the Twin Towers and the Pentagon. With only that knowledge, they made the ultimate decision to intercede on behalf of others. They were determined to alter the outcome of their flight and of history.

In their heroic decision to take back control of the plane, they sacrificed themselves on behalf of others. The passengers and crew had served the greater good of humanity. In the eyes of God, they had committed the ultimate sacrifice, laying down their lives in order to protect their fellow humans. I believe this is why the angels appeared on the field. They arrived to honor the brave men and women on the plane and to transport their souls to God's heavenly realm. They had come to the earthly domain to assist as the lines were drawn between good and evil. Just as the Saints had arisen from their graves after the crucifixion of Jesus, the angels had appeared to escort the souls of God's faithful departed servants aboard Flight 93. The angels had done so to pay homage to the passengers and crew and to revel in the glory of the meaning of their death. Their selfless act of heroism had redeemed our lives and improved the overall well-being of humankind.

CHAPTER

16

THE DARK NIGHT
OF THE SOUL

All my life I have had the grace of God with me. When I was young, I did not comprehend the magnitude of the concept; I just thought I was lucky in some way. On occasion, I was blessed by the presence of the Archangel Michael. No matter the life issue or negative circumstance I faced, it was always resolved for me through divine intervention. I heard that familiar voice whisper in my right ear—advice on how to handle a given situation or a warning of some danger that lay ahead. It took time for me to trust that God would provide. This understanding moved itself into the light of wisdom. It is wonderful to know we are watched over by our guardian angels, that each of us has a direct line of communication to the divine. Our angels are constantly with us to guide, protect, and heal. We need only to tap into their presence.

I learned this truth during some of the most trying moments of my tenure as a police officer. Only now do I fully comprehend the magnitude of my guardian angels' presence in my life. I recall an incident in 1992 during the riots in Los Angeles. On the very night of the ending of the Rodney King case—and the acquittal of the Los Angeles police officers—a series of violent incidents rocked our small community in Pennsylvania.

While on patrol, the officers on duty received a call from emergency dispatch. A couple was trapped inside their vehicle. A group of males had surrounded them and were pummeling the car with rocks. The terrorized couple had contacted the emergency center using their cell phone. The dispatcher requested assistance from any available officer cruising the area.

I happened to be nearby; I advised dispatch that I would respond. Upon arrival, I saw the car in the middle of the roadway, surrounded by men. The men were rocking the car. I contacted dispatch to confirm that there was a problem, and requested immediate backup. I then drove my patrol car in front of the couple's car, catching the attention of the men. Soon a rock shattered the windshield of my car. I put the car in reverse and backed down the street hastily. The males gave chase, allowing the couple to drive away from the scene.

As these events transpired, I kept hearing the sergeant on the radio directing my actions. A short while later, we were redirected to the community housing nearby, as the dispatcher had received complaints of gunfire and vandalism. The sergeant instructed us to contain those who were causing the disturbance. All the officers on duty in the neighboring communities responded as backup.

When we arrived, I heard shots being fired and then saw the streetlights go out. It was dark, and the street felt ominous. I remember taking my shotgun out of the car and putting on a riot helmet. All of us were already wearing flak jackets underneath our police uniforms. We were told to move out, to be careful, and to be in constant radio communication with one another. I moved in the direction of where I heard the gunfire. It was dark and hard to detect any traces of movement by others. All at once, I heard a familiar voice—the voice of the archangel guardian—whisper in my ear, "Watch out behind you."

I turned just in time to see a man coming toward me. All of a sudden, another man appeared from out of nowhere and knocked the perpetrator to the ground. As both men fell onto the asphalt, I heard the one man say to the other, "Oh no, you don't hurt our police officer."

Even amid the tumult of the evening, my heart was filled with warmth upon hearing the words of this dear man. This wonderful savior of the dark night had called me *his* police officer. I knew then I had served my community well. The time spent chatting with the residents and teaching in the schools had somehow strengthened the bond between me and those I was sworn to protect and serve.

Within minutes the other officers arrived and the perpetrator was placed under arrest. I thanked my earthly angel for his bravery and gave him a hug. After we had cleared the incident, I was in the patrol car and the sergeant pulled up next to me. He asked about my well-being and I about his.

He then said, "I'm worried that you have become complacent about dangerous situations."

"What do you mean?" I replied, perplexed.

"When you were calling dispatch to report that your windshield had been shattered," he said, "you were as calm as if you were ordering a pizza." I reflected for a moment and smiled.

"I was never in danger," I said. "My angel is always at my side." He looked at me in an odd way and just shook his head.

Later that night, I remembered the sergeant's words and gave thanks to God. Once again he had delivered me from danger; he had sent my guardian angel. Out of this dangerous night, my soul had once again been delivered from darkness to light. As I traveled throughout the rest of my career, these moments of fully knowing "all will be well regardless" have inspired me. They have helped me trudge through and have wiped my soul clean.

A few days later, I once again saw the man who had rescued me from danger. I gave him another hug and reiterated my gratitude.

He replied, "You are the only police officer who stops in the community and talks to all of us. You are not just here when there is trouble. You spend time with our children so they get to know you as a person. I appreciate how much you care."

On that dark and disturbing night, there had been a great revelation. A rebirth had taken place. My faith in others had been restored, and my belief in my guardian angels was strengthened. I knew without question that my celestial protectors were nearby and whispering in my ear. They were there to guide and protect me as I did the same for my fellow man.

CHAPTER
17

THE FBI
MEETS FEMA

In early March 2008, I traveled to Durango, Colorado, to visit the man in my life. Over the past months my visits with him had brought me some solace. His lovely home by the river and the scenery of the surrounding mountains allowed for some healing to occur. While there I met with a representative from the Federal Emergency Management Agency (FEMA). A mutual friend had arranged the meeting. Although he had been stationed in New York after 9/11, he was now living in the area. He was on medical leave and had moved to Colorado to be closer to a pulmonary clinic in Denver. The lung ailment from which he suffered was directly linked to the "white powder" that had spread throughout New York City after the fall of the Twin Towers.

It seemed that his illness was the result of prolonged exposure to the toxic conditions at Ground Zero.

As we talked, I asked more about his illness, and he told me there were some 70,000 registered victims afflicted with the white powder symptoms. The condition had become common among the first responders and residents of New York City in the months and years following 9/11. The illness had swept across the city and affected many, just like the dust after the fall of the mighty towers.

When I first met this man, I extended my hand to say hello. His grip was strong against mine, but as I looked into his eyes, I immediately recognized a pain that I had seen so often in my own. In his lovely green eyes, there peered a mirror of sadness, interwoven with a knowledge that life would never be the same.

We spent the next couple of hours talking about the events of 9/11, his illness, and the resulting PTSD from which he suffered. He told me about being at Ground Zero and the initial impact it had had on him. He had spent so much time there. I was almost embarrassed to tell him my story after listening to his. When I said as much to him, he looked at me sternly.

"You, too, have been injured," he said. "If what you saw at the site injured your heart and your mind then you, too, are one of the walking wounded. There is no standard as to who was hurt more."

With these words, my tears began to flow. I told him the entire story—and included the angels. He related that he, too, had felt a presence at Ground Zero. He believed that the forces of good were present as the responders and recovery workers lifted body after body from the site. For a brief moment as he spoke, I thought I saw his eyes well up with tears. At that point I knew him to be a kindred spirit.

He shared the awareness of possibilities beyond this earthly domain. I left him hoping that I would have the opportunity to meet with him again. In the meantime, I prayed for a miracle to restore his health.

I'm not sure if this man will ever fully comprehend the gift he gave me that afternoon. In his willingness to share his story and listen to mine, he gave me a release. Even as a man, he was willing to admit that he had been affected by the events of 9/11. He had suffered tremendously at Ground Zero. He had experienced great pain and had kept his secret quiet for far too long. He also shared with me that he had a "saving grace" in his life: one of his co-workers and friends had extended his hand and helped lift him out of the dark abyss of his own tortured mind.

I was truly in awe of this man. His revelation had helped me to heal in some way from the self-incrimination of being a woman who suffered from PTSD. I realized that somewhere deep inside, I had believed I had gotten PTSD because I was a woman. Knowing that he, a man, had experienced something similar released me from the shame I felt. In that moment of recognition, he had saved me.

He, too, had the knowledge of the great black abyss. He understood me, because he had peered into the same dark hole. My heart cried out to his, for I knew I was luckier than he. This wonderful man, who had served his country so loyally, had to bear the knowledge that he may soon die. His doctors said he might have only a few more years. Yet even with his knowledge that death might lurk around the next corner, he was able to share and give comfort to a woman with a broken heart, a woman he barely knew. I am grateful to my fellow patriot and thank him for his mentorship of me. I pray for his recovery and a long life with many years of happiness ahead.

CHAPTER

18

A VOICE IN THE WILDERNESS

One morning in early May 2008, I was very upset with myself. I had been pondering whether or not to resign from the FBI. I was having a rough time deciding which road to take. Should I speak out and tell the world about God's field of angels? Should I maintain my call to service and continue to risk my health? Should I put a request in to the Pittsburgh Division Management for medical leave (as my physicians had recommended)? Should I just take an early retirement and find other gainful employment?

I liked the idea of retirement, but as the woman at FBI headquarters reminded me, I would not be retiring from this job. I would, in fact, be "severing my employment" with the FBI. A harsh term indeed. How do you sever a 25-year career? It felt as if I were severing a limb from my body. Would I become as lifeless as a severed limb? Would I just hang there, unable to reach for the next opportunity? Would I be incapable of any future success? I had all these thoughts churning in my mind and was still no closer to making a decision. So, as in the past, I called to God and asked Him to give me a sign. I wanted Him to guide me.

As I drove to the office, I whispered a prayer. I asked for a clear sign telling me what direction I was to follow. On this particular morning, I was scheduled to assist in co-coordinating an annual "Tension Task Force" meeting with the Pennsylvania Human Relations Commission (PHRC). The meeting was going to be conducted in the Pittsburgh Field Office. This annual meeting provided an opportunity to convene representatives from a diverse group of agencies, all of whom were tasked with addressing civil rights issues. These agencies had been meeting for ten years, ever since a series of tragic events in the greater Pittsburgh area. The meeting ran its usual course. There was a great deal of discussion regarding the racial tensions in the schools. There were many comments about the current elections and the role they were playing in youth behavioral patterns. There was an awful lot of conjecture and very little resolution. As was my tendency when a meeting was becoming too bureaucratic in nature, I spoke up. I indicated that we were missing an important issue. We were not here to boast about our agency or how great we each were. We were here to discuss matters that would serve in the best interest of our children.

As I finished my soapbox oratory, the regional director for the PHRC requested that I join him at the podium. I walked toward him hesitantly. As I got closer, I noticed that he was taking out a plaque from underneath the podium.

"We have an award for you," he said. "This award is the first of its kind. It was created just for you. You have been the voice to be reckoned with. You have said the words that needed to be expressed. You have worked tirelessly to get the job done and have succeeded in coordinating an army of agencies.

"The award," he went on, "is entitled A Voice in the Wilderness."

I was shocked. As I turned to him, he placed the award in my reluctant hands.

"Is this a nice way of saying that I have a big mouth?" I asked.

The room erupted with laughter and humorous comments. I looked around at all of the familiar faces and I smiled. How lucky I felt to be in the midst of such wonderful and dedicated individuals. Each of these lovely creatures was a rare gem in our tumultuous society. I thanked the PHRC for the honor of the award and for the privilege of working with each of the meeting's attendees. I accepted it on behalf of all of the wonderful agency representatives who had worked alongside me all those years.

In that moment of thanksgiving, it occurred to me that I had received my sign. I had been given another gift. I had been graced not only by the award but also by a sign from above. God had given me the guidance I so desired. The term *voice in the wilderness* had taken on two meanings. The phrase on the plaque not only referred to a job well done. I also saw it as a sign that the time had arrived for me to speak my truth to the world. It was time to share the story of the angels. For it was in the wilderness of that stark landfill that I had heard the cry of the lone hawk. The hawk had announced the presence of the angels; it was the reminder that the spirit of God was all around us. He was there in that moment of crisis, when the world cried to Him for help. That story needed a strong voice in order to be heard. I had heard the cry in the wilderness. That day, the wasteland of my heart was filled. I knew my future purpose. I was ready to respond to God's call to service.

CHAPTER

19

SUPERWOMAN HAS
LEFT THE ROOM

Between 2005 and 2008, I spent many days in therapy. I did so willingly, but only half believing that I was suffering from an illness. At this time, I was not yet ready to accept the diagnosis of PTSD or its impact on my health. In fact, I was having a hard time truly grasping the concept of the illness. On one of my first visits to a new psychotherapist, I had the opportunity to discuss with the doctor the definition of PTSD. She gently queried if any of my treating medical professionals had shared the clinical definition of the illness. I explained that no one had given me such information. She then inquired if I would care to read from the medical book that provided the official terminology used to describe and diagnose the illness to insurance providers. I indicated that being a visual learner, it might be helpful to read the information. So she handed me the little red book that was opened at a particular page, and I began to read from it. As I read the list of symptoms, I asked the doctor how many were necessary to diagnose the illness. She said that two or more symptoms needed to be present. I began to laugh out loud. The doctor was surprised at my response and asked about it. I related I was just laughing at the fact that I had all of the symptoms *except* for two.

I then began to cry.

"For the rest of my life," I said, "I am going to be labeled as a psychiatric patient."

"Yes," replied the doctor, gently, "by some you will be. However, as all health professionals are aware, PTSD is the only psychiatric illness that starts with a traumatic injury."

I was not very comforted by her words. I knew all too well what the label would mean in my profession. There would be no sympathy from my fellow law enforcement officers. I would be perceived as the woman who "went over the edge." I feared I would lose my credibility, becoming the woman who couldn't take the pressure of the job. It would be just like my first months as a police officer when the men repeatedly taunted me about being female. I had heard all too many times how women do not belong in policing. That we are the weaker sex and incapable of doing the job. I had become engaged in all too many arguments in those early years. Now, as I pondered those conversations and disputes, I realized women *did* belong in the world of law enforcement. The industry *needs* us to retain our identity, our female essence.

However, I had not done that. I'd created two distinct personas—a professional front and a softer side that was only apparent to those who truly knew and cared for me.

In the latter days of my career, I had often said to the men, "I came into this profession as a nice girl, and I'm leaving it as a woman I hardly recognize." This was the harsh reality of my almost 25 years in the profession. Sitting in that therapist's office that day, I realized that Superwoman had finally learned her lesson and had now left the room.

Her leaving made me feel a sense of great loss and sadness. How humbling it was to know that, in order to heal, I would have to shed my professional persona and retrieve the remnants of the soft woman from days gone by. Superwoman had been my identity for so long. I had worn her uniform with pride. My ego, my fidelity, my integrity, and my bravery were all interwoven into her cape. Yet I had also worn it to shield myself from the world. Every piece of material and each thread that created the red, white, and blue patchwork of my cape had intertwined into it some aspect of my personality. Nestled underneath that cape lay the essence of a wounded woman who had somehow given up on her life.

I was still capable and functional with my work. I knew very well the meaning of overachieving. But, just like an alcoholic, I had been in denial for too long. And when it came to my personal life, I had become immobilized by fear. My inability to let go of the past had overburdened my heart and my mind, and I had lost the desire to reach out toward the future. As I removed my symbolic uniform and cape, I asked my old persona—Lillie—to return. I hoped that somewhere deep inside me she was still present and waiting to reemerge. I wondered whether she had survived, and just how much of her had remained intact. I was hopeful that, through the various therapies I was about to undertake, she would feel safe to come back to life. I wanted her to be a shining beacon of light as I moved through the next phases of healing.

In those first few glimpses of self-recognition and admission of my fear, I saw pieces of my puzzled self as I used to be. I had a decision to make. Did I really want to live, or did I want to die?

If I chose life, a hard road lay ahead. Days would be filled with doctors' appointments, medications, the possible loss of my job and my income, shame, pain, sorrow, regret, and alienation from those I had loved and worked so closely with. I would be leaving behind my comrades in arms. Or, more to the point, they would trail away from me. Then, there were my family and friends. How would they react? Would they be willing to support me in my time of need? If I chose death, on the other hand, all I needed to do was give in to the pain within. My mind and body would wear away with neglect and time. Given my current state of health, it would be an easier road to travel.

I looked in the mirror for any glimmer of an answer. To my surprise, I heard a reply. A gentle voice said to me, "Live, prosper, and succeed." I recognized the strong yet soft tone of the voice as that of my father. I felt the tears well up. Emotion rose from deep in my soul and surged upward to my throat. I heard my own voice cry out, "Elohim, Elohim, Elohim, please rescue me from this wasteland and restore me to my destiny. I cannot do this on my own."

In my moment of requiem, a stirring rose in my soul. I was moved toward my redemption and the light. What I thought would be my swan song had become my aria of saving grace.

CHAPTER

20

A SECRET REVEALED

On September 11, 2007, I had been invited to serve as a guest speaker for the annual 9/11 anniversary mass at St. Thomas More University Parish in Indiana, Pennsylvania. I had received the invitation from a mutual friend of a colleague who served with the Pennsylvania Emergency Management Agency. Although I had agreed to speak, I was very hesitant. I contemplated the possibility of revealing my entire story—angels included—in front of a congregation of people I did not know. I spent the days leading up to the presentation pondering what was appropriate to say. Was it the right time to share God's message with a group of virtual strangers? Was it a good idea to reveal it in the church setting? Was I not a sinner and still tainted with the sins of my thoughts and deeds? Did I dare speak—and open myself to rebuke?

As the day approached, I contacted an old friend who also happened to be a publicist. She and I had known each other since our days in junior high school—almost 40 years! Though we rarely had contact with each other, when we did speak it was as if no time had passed. She had secured a place in my heart for being one of the true friends in my life. She was one of the few who had supported me and not abandoned me when I became pregnant at a young age. She stood by my side and helped me stay strong in my convictions about the situation. We had a great deal in common, and our personalities were similar in design.

One of my favorite moments with her happened on my wedding day. Dinner had just been served to some three hundred guests, all of whom were quietly eating their food, when the main doors of the reception hall swung open. The doors unexpectedly slammed against the walls to either side, causing all eyes in the room to look up. There, standing in the entrance to the hall, stood my friend in all of her glory—and embarrassment. Seeing that all eyes were now upon her, she attempted to back out of the door. Instead, I caught her eye, and I gestured for her to come see me up on the stage. (In typical Italian style, the bride, groom, wedding party, and parents were all seated on a stage above the guests.) With some hesitation, my friend approached. As she climbed the stairs to where I sat, all eyes were still on her. When she finally made her way to me, we embraced and laughed.

She then said, "Now, I know how Moses felt when he parted the Red Sea. I just parted the Great White Sea, and it was pretty scary."

It took me a minute to realize what exactly she had meant. But as I looked out at all of the faces of the guests, I realized she was the only African American in the room!

Our laughter was contagious, and soon the entire bridal party had joined in. I so admired my friend's tenacity. In an extreme moment of discomfort, she had prevailed through the gift of levity. No wonder she had chosen a profession as a publicist. Even at her youthful age, she proved that she could handle herself in any situation.

It was the same reason I chose to reach out to her for help all these years later. I needed her comfort, her help, and her unique brand of magic. I called her in the days leading up to the speech and told her everything that had happened since 9/11. After explaining the field of angels, I laid out my present dilemma. I asked for her professional advice. Should I talk about the angels? As I'd hoped, she had wonderful suggestions. She also offered to travel with me to the church on the day of the speech to provide her support.

When the evening of the presentation arrived, I was filled with trepidation. It was an unnerving 90 minutes in the car. The anniversary date of 9/11 had always made me feel anxious, and on this particular night I was filled with a high level of anxiety. All too soon, we arrived at the church. As we drove through the parking lot, I saw that it was filled to capacity. I became very apprehensive; there were going to be many more people sitting in the pews than I had at first imagined.

As we walked into the church, my eyes scanned the pews, which were now filled with people. I hesitated at the door, but my friend put her hand on my shoulder and gently guided me into the vestibule. Her gentle touch gave me some comfort. Before too long I regained some composure, and a moment later we were whisked away to be introduced to the parish priest. As I spoke to the priest about my intended presentation, I felt a quiet calm take hold of me. I again pondered my choice to reveal the entire story. I gave the priest a brief description of the events of 9/11, including the angel visitation, and asked for his thoughts. The priest placed his hand on my shoulder and explained that I didn't need his guidance. God had already guided me to the church, he said, and it was quite possible that my story would promote healing for myself and others. It was then that I felt a huge burden lift from my soul. I had indeed arrived at this very destination by God's design. Was it the moment to begin some type of healing? Was it the moment of revelation? If indeed it was, what did I fear? Was it not God's story and that of His angels?

Within minutes, we walked down the aisle to an empty pew, and I genuflected. Then, I noticed that some of the men were dressed in their Knights of Columbus regalia. I was very familiar with this distinctive clothing because my own father had been a member of this prestigious corps of men. As I peered at the faces of these men, I saw an image of my dad lying in his coffin wearing his Knights of Columbus uniform. He had been laid to rest wearing his black tuxedo, crisply ironed white shirt, red sash, and cherished saber. The memory of Dad and his affection for the association quieted the restlessness in me. A peace entered my soul, and I felt a calming energy take hold. I knew instinctively that it was time to release the story, if for no other reason than to honor my dad and the men in the room who had shared his vocation as a member of the royal knights of the church.

When it was my time to speak, I rose to my feet and slowly walked to the altar. Before I could give it any thought, the words began to exit my mouth. The story flowed with such ease. The motion in the room slowed down, and in my mind's eye I saw the visions of the Shanksville field. With each new phrase I uttered, the ropes that had bound my heart for so long began to untangle themselves. I felt an indescribable joy coming from the recesses of my soul; I had to still the urge to scream an *alleluia*. Soon the tears began to fall from my eyes. I looked at my friend and she was crying, too.

As I finished my talk and I moved to leave the altar, the entire congregation rose to its feet. The room erupted in a standing ovation. I knew the real reason for the congregation's reaction. It was in praise of God and His divine sign of grace. It was for the angels who had shown themselves on the field. And most especially, it was to recognize the heroic deeds of the brave men and women who had perished on Flight 93. As I walked back to my seat, I felt a deep stirring of pride. I had done something that had seemed impossible. In this beautiful and simply decorated church, in front of a group of people I did not know, I had shared a story that had lain dormant inside me for so long. I had feared a negative reaction but instead received heartfelt recognition. For the first time in a very long time, I felt as if I had stood up and regained my voice.

Before I left the church that night, many congregants came to me with stories of their own encounters with angels. As I listened, I reflected upon the many blessings in all our lives. In the most trying moments, many of us are fortunate enough to be visited and touched by angels. These angels serve as our guides and our protectors. I had entered the church fearful of the unknown and once again had received a visitation of angels. This time it was not the winged celestial visitors I had witnessed in Shanksville but the many kind and caring members of the parish. I left the church with renewed courage and direction. I had been restored with a new sense of purpose and hope for the life ahead.

As I left the church that evening, I was given two lovely gifts. The parish priest gave me a cross that he had carried with him from Jerusalem. As I touched the cross, a warm feeling spread into my hand. The cross, already a sacred article in my faith, had been brought from the holiest of locations in the Middle East. It was an excellent reminder of my faith and the suffering that Jesus had endured in order to provide resurrection to us all. It reminded me that the conviction in one's faith is the very backbone of one's soul. As I held the cross in my hand, a female parishioner approached and gifted me with a prayer shawl she had knitted herself. When she placed the delicately knitted shawl in my hands, my heart rippled and my battered mind exhaled. The cross now hangs on the wall of my grandchildren's playroom. There it watches over the children as they play—a reminder of God's grace and light. On occasion I retrieve the prayer shawl from its hiding place. As I unwrap it and place it on my shoulders, it reminds me of God's protection and helps alleviate any fears I might have.

The memory of that evening in the church still burns brightly in my mind. As I close my eyes, the vision of all the parishioners comes easily into view. The handsome men of the Knights of Columbus stand tall in their loyalty to the church, a symbolic reminder of the faith that sustains their lives. The memory of their presence always takes me back to my dad's funeral. There, standing next to his casket, were his fellow Knights. As each person walked to view my dad's remains, the Knights stood guard to illuminate his journey to the golden gates above. They were there to remind Dad that even in death he was not without his comrades in arms. It was a reminder to all present that we are never alone.

A LILY IN BLOOM

Over the next few months as I entered my journey toward healing, I experienced both emotional and physical pain. The physical symptoms seemed to arise in every direction, and I often became fearful when an area of my body would experience a new pain pattern. On the emotional side, one of the most confusing experiences was a sense of lost confidence. This sensation was so new to me, because over the years in my profession I had acquired a strong sense of self and an ability to address almost any situation that arose on both personal and professional levels. But, in recent months, my sense of self-confidence had dissipated with each visit to the doctor and each discussion related to my mental health. The more I thought about the situation, the deeper I fell into a state of anxiety.

In August 2008, I received another gift that temporarily assisted in the restoration of my self-confidence. I was in a rush to make a physical therapy appointment. The morning had been very hectic. A friend had been visiting my home, and he needed a ride to his truck. I was already running late. I made an attempt to reschedule my appointment for later that day, but the receptionist at the therapist's office informed me that there were no other slots available. So I hurried to take my friend to his destination and to make my therapy appointment.

As I was traveling on Route 56 near my home, I approached an intersection in which the traffic light had turned red. As I slowed down, I noticed that a dark-colored SUV traveling ahead of me was not stopping.

Before I knew it, the SUV had driven straight through the intersection, where it struck a truck. The truck stopped on impact, and the SUV swerved slightly to the left. I immediately drove to the vicinity of the vehicles and parked my car on the side of the road. I exited my car and ran to the truck first. Inside the truck sat two men, both of whom appeared to be all right. Both were talking on their cell phones. I asked about their well-being and whether they had called 911. I recognized one of the men as an old family friend. Both of them indicated that they were fine and that the police had been notified. I then moved to the SUV and noticed that there was a great deal of smoke coming from the vehicle. As I looked inside the SUV, I heard a woman screaming that her car was on fire. I told her I was there to help and she should calm down and turn off the engine. I asked if she was injured and then noticed that there was also a small boy sitting in a safety seat in the rear of the vehicle.

I opened the rear door of the SUV and asked the little boy if he was hurt.

"No," he responded. "I'm not hurt, but I'm scared."

"I'm scared, too," I said. "But we need to get you and your mom out of the car." I asked if he would allow me to help him out of the car, and he nodded. I did a quick pat-down of the child to make sure there were no apparent injuries and advised the woman that I was going to remove her son from the car. She gave me permission, and I gently lifted the boy from his safety seat. As I was lifting him, the woman again began to scream that her vehicle was on fire. I quickly reacted and instructed her to move to the rear of the vehicle and climb out the back door. I explained that both of the front doors were damaged and could not be opened. I then carried her son to the side of the road. The woman soon followed behind us. As I carried the boy to a safe place, I noticed that there were chemicals spilling from the SUV onto the roadway.

It was only a few minutes later that the police officers arrived at the scene and took charge of the situation. I recognized one of the officers, and he asked if I had been involved in the accident. I explained that I had witnessed the incident. I then gave the police officers my version of the accident and left to go to my therapy appointment.

In the moments that followed, I heard that familiar voice inside my ear. The voice indicated that I had received three gifts on that day. The three gifts were as follows: The first was the reminder that God is indeed in control of the dominoes in my life. All of us live in His design. If I had arrived there a few minutes earlier or a few minutes later, I would not have been at the accident scene. It was a reminder that God has supreme control of my destiny.

The second gift was something that proved the doctors had indeed been right about the way the PTSD would respond to a new traumatic event. My doctors had told me that because of prior conditioning, my body would instantly release endorphins. And it was true. Almost immediately upon seeing the accident I'd felt a sense of euphoria running through my body. Adrenaline surged through my veins, and I felt wonderful and relaxed. This feeling of relaxation was the direct opposite of the anxiety I had felt for the past few years.

The third gift was the momentary return of my self-confidence. In those first moments following the crash, I saw how capable I was. My training kicked into high gear, and it was "showtime" once again. I hadn't lost my ability to serve my fellow human beings. I was still capable of helping someone in need. I was still a viable human being and valuable to our society.

Despite the trauma of the accident, I had been given three new gifts. I drove away from the scene feeling much better about myself and my life. It truly was a blessed day. Not only did God save four people from any major injuries, He also restored my sense of self-worth.

Three days later, one of my prized calla lilies bloomed for the first time in three years. Its vibrant flame color went from deep lemon yellow at the center to red at the edges, all against the green plume of its leaves. In my mind, it was a symbolic gesture of the dominoes again falling into place, since the lily had not bloomed in three years. I viewed the bloom as a sign of new life about to begin—not only for my prized plant but for me as well.

CHAPTER

22

WEEDING THROUGH

As I moved through the various stages of the healing process, I would periodically use the Archangel Oracle Cards that I had purchased during a visit to a health spa. These beautifully designed cards are part of a collection developed by Doreen Virtue, a renowned psychologist and author who works very closely with the angelic realm in her healing practice. The cards became a form of release for me. Almost every time I used the deck, I pulled the Archangel Jophiel card. The card was inscribed with the words "Clear Your Space." The lovely card, with its alluring depiction of the archangel, reminds the reader to "Get rid of the clutter, clear the energy around you." Each time I would hold the card in my hand I would ask, *What clutter?* How many more closets, cupboards, dresser drawers, and storage boxes could I rummage through?

There were not many spaces left in my small home that I had not ripped apart over the past few months. But again and again I would pull that same card from the pile. I was reminded that the archangels were more knowledgeable than I. Obviously they were trying to get my attention about something!

As I continued to rummage through my home, my belongings, and the mementos of my life, I finally realized what message the archangel was trying to deliver. It had nothing to do with my physical space and everything to do with the cluttered spaces around my heart and my mind. Both of these vital parts of me were clogged with innumerable memories. As I became more aware of the card's meaning for me, I realized that my heart and mind had been filled to the brim like one of those portable storage containers. And inside the locked container of my heart and mind lay the remnants of the past.

It was necessary to look into those memories before the present time would make any sense and the future would have a chance to manifest. These memories had remained dormant in the dark corners of my mind and the hidden spaces of my heart. If I was to truly heal, I would need to clear out the debris. So I began to peel open the many compartments in my mind, peering into those events in my life that had stopped the process of healing.

I knew I had to start with the very first moments of that September day. I had to inch my way to the place where the debris had begun to build. I had to take hold of that place in order to ultimately take back my life.

I needed to understand why I continued to hoard all those memories, why I allowed them to remain. If I intended to heal from the trauma, I had to know where I had become frozen with fear. It was time to weed through all the leftover memories that remained ingrained inside my psyche and finally let go of the past events. If I could accomplish this, I could eradicate the rubbish that needed to be discarded. If I could successfully "clear my space," there would be room for healing and spiritual growth.

CHAPTER
23

THE SOUTHWEST TRAIL

In October 2007, I made another trip to Durango, Colorado. On this particular trip, I traveled not only to Durango but also to other areas in the Southwest as well. As I ventured to each new location, I was constantly aware of the vastness of the mountain ranges. The ranges varied not only in size, shape, coloration, and contour, but in the quality of their energy. Some of them had very subtle and soothing energy. It moved lightly and mixed ever so gently with the wind. Some of the ranges had heavy energy that swirled with the movement of air. I could actually sense the density of it as it pressed against my skin. I could feel it with each breath through my nostrils, as it moved across and through the recesses of my body. It felt invigorating and alive. My senses were keen. My hope was everlasting. My desire to communicate and express my emotions became an important part of each day. The clarity of thought moved me in ways I had not sensed prior to this experience. Before my trips to the Southwest, I had heard stories from my friends about the magnificence of the mountains and the energy that they contained. Now, as I traveled through the mountain ranges, across the plains and deserts, I understood what they had meant.

A short time into my return journey to Durango, I observed what I believed were the forms of angels on the tops of various mountain ranges. They appeared only upon the rugged contours of the mountaintops. Each form stood on the rough edge of a peak with its arms extended toward the sky. I saw the forms in a very abstract way, surrounded by hues of lavender and blue. At first glance, the form appeared to be human. Yet it was obscure enough that identifying its definitive shape was not possible. I knew that this was a sign sent from God and that it had special meaning for me.

It took about a month for me to realize what the visions of the angels on the mountain ranges had meant. It was a cold Thanksgiving afternoon back in Pennsylvania. The weather was gloomy, and I was feeling somewhat depressed. My PTSD was kicking in and once again I worried about the outcome of another episode. As my mood worsened, I knelt down to pray. I recall asking God for help with the sudden mood changes. As I raised my hands to the Heavens, I immediately sensed that which had eluded me regarding the vision on the mountain peaks. It had not been merely an angel I had seen. The vision was symbolic of a *human being,* rising to the essence of its higher power. The image was that of a human, raising its hands to the

Heavens—calling to God and seeking the universal energy of the mountains. The louder the person's cries, the more the universal energy began to move across the sky. As the form moved to outstretch its arms, a metamorphosis took place. From the depths of the earth, a softness of feathered wings began to develop. The figure's arms began to transform into angel wings. The pale-blue color of the sky was shrouded by the shimmers and bursts of brilliant blue and purple hues of the celestial form. Both the angelic and the human forms became one, the natural light of the sky intermixed with the radiance and purity of spiritual white light above the extended arms.

The message of the vision had such clarity and affirmation. This magnificent image was another gift from God. It would serve as a reminder that, as human beings, we are constantly evolving toward our higher power. Most of us consistently strive toward bettering ourselves. After all, is prayer not the heightened words and thoughts of our inner selves? Is not prayer the very act of bettering ourselves, while asking for help in doing so? The human-to-angel metamorphosis was the best manner in which to depict these thoughts and the meaning of the vision. It would serve as a reminder to each of us to respond to the deeper yearnings of our souls. It would be one of the lasting images of God's message in my story. It would serve as testimony that good does conquer evil. It is a lasting message of hope, trust, and God's greatest gift of love for all of His children.

At my moment of recognition that Thanksgiving day, it was apparent to me that the form was pointing the way toward my future path. It was the passage of my destiny. My fear of disclosure had dissipated. My need to hide the truth was gone. It was now time to open my mind and heart and allow the world to know of my story about the field of angels on that fateful September day. It was finally time to leap off the ledge and allow the net to appear. I should no longer worry about the outcome, for I knew the integrity of the message would reign supreme. Those who chose to believe would be comforted by the message. They would know the truth of my journey. They would recognize their own story and belief within mine. I could no longer worry about nonbelievers; theirs was not my journey. My journey was to provide the testimony of the angels in the field. It was my responsibility to carry God's message to the believers and seekers of His truth. It was my duty to regain my strength of courage and composure in order to deliver His message to those who were willing to hear.

LIFE'S PURPOSE

"Does anyone think that victory is possible without facing danger?"

This is a quote from the latest version of a movie about Pearl Harbor. It came to mind one evening as I sat contemplating my life's purpose. I was thinking about the reason for my life, as well as for the lives of the passengers and crew members aboard Flight 93. *What was my life's purpose?* I asked myself, and *would I be able to fulfill my sacred contract?* I could identify at least two reasons for my existence. I did know that, first and foremost, I was born to be a mother and bring my daughter into this world. She, in turn, would deliver her three daughters and her son into the world and would serve as a beacon of guiding light on their behalf. Motherhood was certainly the most important function of my life. But what else was I here for?

In these quiet moments of contemplation I explored the content of my life through questions. Had I truly helped others to improve their lives? Had my life had any positive effect on those whom I loved? Had I helped others to reach a level of excellence? My father had often explained that it was important to know that you walked the earth to help others achieve their goals in life. It was important to become a person of quality and then to assist others on their journeys as well.

In 1984, in the early stages of my law enforcement career, I found a beautiful little news clip about the life of Benjamin Franklin. A man had written an article about Mr. Franklin in which he'd asked him about his apparent wealth and material gain.

"It was not a true test of a man's character if he had acquired great wealth or property," Mr. Franklin reportedly replied. "It is, however, a true testimony of one's character if they have been responsible for positively affecting at least one person's life for the better."

When I first came across this little anecdote, I cut it out and taped it on the inside of my locker in the squad room. Each tour of duty, as I opened my locker, this message was the first thing I would see. I read it every day as a reminder of my place in the world as a member of the law enforcement profession. I was there to serve and protect. I was there to help others in a time of need. I was there to give guidance and strength when necessary.

On my first day as a police officer, I experienced an embarrassing moment with my new partner that would turn into a life lesson from my dear father. As I was getting dressed at home, I made repeated attempts to buckle my new gun belt into place. Having no success, I lost my redheaded temper and began cursing at it—without notic-ing that my mom was standing in my bedroom doorway.

"Lillie Marie," she asked, startled. "Who are you yelling at?"

"I'm angry at this damn gun belt," I responded, gruffly. "I can't get the clasp to fasten."

She looked at me rather innocently and asked, "Why don't you get the other officer to help you with the belt when he gets here?"

I looked up at her in disbelief.

"Great idea, Mom. He can just help dress the incom-petent woman. That should make him feel real confident about my abilities. How could he believe that I could han-dle policing if I can't even buckle a damn belt?"

"You know I don't like it when you swear," she said.

Mumbling something else I couldn't quite hear, she shrugged her shoulders and left the room. I realized it was about time for my partner to pick me up, so I hurriedly grabbed the rest of my gear and ran from my room. I got downstairs and opened the front door where, to my sur-prise, my partner stood already waiting for me. He was talk-ing with both of my parents. My dad seemed to be rapidly firing a multitude of questions at him. It took everything in me not to remind my dad that my partner had not arrived at the house to take me on a date; he was there to drive me to *work*. I stilled the need to express the sarcasm and said hello.

My partner looked up at me and smiled.

"Your mother tells me you're having a tough time fas-tening your gun belt to your pants," he said. "Why don't you come over here and let me see if I can help you with it? Don't be embarrassed. It happened to all of us when we first tried to adjust it. I promise I won't tell anybody that I helped you get dressed. It will be our secret."

I should have known the secret would not be left just between us. In fact, this scene would be revisited for many years to come. It was shared with many a police officer when my partner felt the need to poke fun at the rookie he had helped to groom into a cop.

He burst into laughter, and I felt my face go flush. I glanced over at my mom and gave her an angry look. She again shrugged her shoulders and walked inside the house. I hesitantly walked over to him and handed him the gun belt. With one quick movement of his hands, the belt was snapped into place. As the snugly fit leather fastened around my waist, I looked up at him and thanked him for his assistance. He again just smiled at me and said nothing in return. I was grateful for his silence.

After spending these embarrassing moments with both my mother and father, my partner and I began to walk toward the patrol car. Before I reached the sidewalk, however, my dad requested a private moment with me. He politely asked my partner to wait for me in the patrol car, opened the front door of our home, and requested that I come inside for a quiet moment of reflection. We entered the kitchen and my dad asked me to turn to him and look in his eyes. I did as he requested.

"I'm not sure I agree with your choice of a job," he said. "I'm not sure I want one of my daughters working as a police officer. That said, I want you to know that I am proud of you. You have always had the eye of the tiger. However, if you choose to begin today, there are a few rules that go along with this new job. If you are agreeable to these rules, I'll approve of your choice."

I nodded my head in agreement and listened as Dad continued.

"These are the rules. First, if you ever start acting like the men and lose your femininity, you have to quit. Never forget your God-given talents as a woman. If you ever start behaving like the men and swearing, you have to quit the job. Never forget for one minute from where you came and that it's only through the grace of God and the fact that you had good parents that you turned out so well. In other words, girl, if you arrest the prostitute on the street tonight, make sure you are polite to her the next time you meet."

Finishing the terms of his conditions, Dad asked me if I was agreeable to these rules. I nodded my head and said, "Yes." He then gave me one of his famous bear hugs, kissed me on the forehead, and told me to go. Before I walked out of the door, I stopped in front of the statue of the Blessed Mother and kissed her on the head. As I genuflected in front of the icon of Mary, I said a silent prayer that She protect and guide me in my newfound career. I got up off my knee and walked out the door and down the stairs to the patrol car. The whole time, I reflected on Dad's words. It would take me a few months to fully comprehend the magnitude of his wisdom. It would take the arrest of a prostitute the first winter I worked. It would take a great deal of ribbing from my fellow male officers. It would take many hard knocks in those first 18 months of policing. It would take the reconciliation of my heart and mind to fully comprehend his words.

What I learned in the intervening years of policing was the importance of a legacy in fulfilling one's life purpose. What we leave behind is our legacy to our families, friends, and the world. What my father left behind was a true legacy as the epitome of a good man, a devoted parent, and a caring educator. Dad's love and kindness were reflected on his last day on this earth as his family stood vigil when he took his last breaths. His legacy was apparent at his funeral, as innumerable people waited in line to view his body and tell us, his wife and children, of Dad's benevolence to them. Some of these people waited for hours to talk to us. These marvelous individuals took the time to come and share their love. They told us about the times Dad bought them food, a coat, or a pair of shoes. They talked about the time he took to correct their behavior or give them accolades for an accomplishment. As each person talked, he or she smiled and often shed tears. Yes, this was the legacy of my father to his wife, children, family, friends, and this world. He had obviously fulfilled his destiny. He left his mark on this world in the very essence of all his kind deeds.

My father would often say that he was not a perfect man and that on any given day he would make mistakes. On this day of remembrance of him, however, his mistakes were not what people remembered. As the casket was closed inside the mausoleum at the cemetery, and as the trumpet played taps, all those present wept a river of tears. As I looked across the room at all the faces, I knew my dad had left his mark on this world. He had left a legacy of honor. Dad had done it in the name of God and humanity. This strong, handsome man, a mixture of kindness and gruffness, had achieved his life's purpose. He had provided the opportunity for others to achieve excellence. I only hope that when my days come to an end, I, too, will have served my purpose and allowed the opportunity for others to shine.

I am sure that a part of my legacy is in recounting the events of 9/11. It is my sacred contract in this lifetime to tell this story. The families of the victims aboard Flight 93, as well, can rest assured that their loved ones have indeed left a legacy behind. It is a legacy of strength of character, bravery, and love. It is a legacy to be told for many generations to come by their children and their children's children, who will hold their heads high in memory of their proud ancestry. May the passengers and crew members aboard Flight 93 rest in peace, knowing that they left an unbelievable legacy of honor behind. All of us who live on through the ages will know of these magnificent men and women who provided for humankind and left their mark on humanity and this world.

A TALE OF
TWO MUSES

A few years ago, a friend who had traveled to Prague gave me a gift of six straw angels. He knew I collected angels and thought I would enjoy these unique tiny dolls made exclusively of cornstalks. He believed they would enhance the angelic collection that was already housed in the various locations of my home. These small and delicate figurines seemed to have a life of their own. They were tiny and fragile in appearance. Yet when held, they emitted great energy and warmth. On my first time holding them, I admired their beauty. As I sat by the river's edge looking at them, I was totally charmed. I instantly felt their energy. As I looked at the faces I heard a voice say, "Give four away and keep two for yourself."

So, over the following year, I did just as I was requested to do. I gradually gave four of the angels to friends and acquaintances, each of whom was having some difficulty in their life. As each of these people accepted an angel into their hand, they commented on feeling an immediate warmth and energy swirling into their palms as they held their tiny angel.

After having given away the four angels, I placed the two that I had kept in my bedroom. I hung one on each side of my headboard. One of the angels held a book in its small hands and the other a set of cymbals. I was curious about the choice of angels that I had coveted for my own safekeeping. Each of them resembled a facet of my life. A facet that not too many people knew existed in my personality. The book depicted the part of me that loves to read and write. I had written down my thoughts and feelings since I was 16 years old. The other equally displayed a hidden side of me. I loved music. It was a piece of me that my mother had given to me. Her love of music had been passed on to me and some siblings. Even though she and I shared little with respect to our chosen paths, she had definitely provided me with the music gene. I wasn't sure if my mom was aware of this. But I hoped in time she would be made aware and pleased with this knowledge.

As I lay in bed each night over the passing years, I could feel the angels' energy, and I could hear their whispers in my ear. On one such night, I heard one of the angels whisper, "Get up and write."

I did as requested, and over the next three weeks, I wrote 20-odd chapters contained in this book.

A few days later, I heard the other angel whisper to me, "Create a song." So, once again I did as I was requested to do. As I stood in the shower that morning, I heard voices singing a song and violins playing in a rhythmic melody. The melodic rhapsody permeated my mind and body and pierced the very recesses of my soul. I then heard my own voice singing the words in the tones of the Gaelic language. The lyrics flowed, as did the song. It was very slow paced and stirring. It lifted my mind to new levels and heights. I watched as my hands and arms were lifted and simulated the playing of the violin. I immediately wrote the words down on paper and captured the melody inside my head. To date, I have sung this song to several individuals and each responds in the same manner. The song stirs deep emotion in those who listen. In the past months, a young composer has brought the song to life. He has worked to complete a lovely composition of angelic design.

It wasn't until a few months following these events that I realized what a wonderful gift I had received from my friend. Not only had he given me the angels to add to my collection; he had given me the gift of two muses. Having these two lovely beings hanging on my headboard had opened up my mind. They had aided in the release of my higher power. They were indeed the muses of music and writing: the muse of writing as portrayed by the angel holding the book, and the muse of music as depicted through the hands of the angel holding the cymbals. They had stirred creativity in me and had helped me channel my God-given, if hidden, talents.

As previously indicated, I had engaged in writing dating back to my teenage years. And in fact, in 1995, when I was home for an extended period of time following surgery, I even created a book of poetry entitled *Thoughts of a Woman Named Trouble*. The book was a compilation of poems I had written throughout my life. But in this long span of time, I had not constructively used this talent. It now appeared that it was time to do so.

As I finished writing the last pages of this book, I took note of the special gifts in my life. I was deeply moved at the knowledge of how the pieces were beginning to fit together. These pieces were being strategically placed like a beautifully constructed mosaic. After all, life *is* a colorful mosaic as one piece fits with another. Life is uniquely sculpted and crafted to create a finished product. If we get it right, we leave this earth knowing we served our time well. Just like one's life, the selected pieces intertwine and segue to precision. One piece tightly fit and bound to the other. So was my life. It emulated the paths so many others have taken before me. All patterned and intersected, weaving their paths across time and space. Life is the many pieces of a puzzle all mixing to become the relevant points of passage. All of these pieces are merged together to a final location and outcome. Our lives lead to our final destination and rebirth. I had been given my rebirth. Out of my pain and suffering, I had emerged triumphant and stronger. In the light of God, I have grown and become a better image to present in front of Him. I hope there is much more life yet ahead. I know there is much more I must strive to improve. However, life now seems so much sweeter and less bitter to the taste.

I am grateful to my muses as they have moved me to reach for new horizons: to a life I had felt was somewhat unfulfilled prior to the writing of my book. In writing this book, I have accomplished a dream I set for myself almost 40 years ago. I have found that life does contain great happiness and joy. I have found my dream in the arms of my Heavenly Father. He has provided me with an ending and a happier path to follow. If for some reason I knew this were my last day on earth, I would leave knowing that I have left my mark. I have left behind a lovely daughter, who thrives and participates in this world. She in turn has borne four children to grow and flourish among us. Like the fine-tuned story of others in our lives, I will leave behind my gift to humanity, and I am ever hopeful I have done as God has asked.

A CHRISTMAS
SHAWL

A few days before Christmas 2008, I received a package that bore the return address of a friend—a colleague who had served with me at the FBI. She and I had shared a genuine relationship that had flourished in my last few years at the Bureau. She had become one of my trusted compatriots and confidantes at work. We shared many a conversation and on occasion gifted each other with meaningful presents.

Our relationship was important to me because my friendships with my fellow employees were somewhat strained. This was especially true regarding my relationships with the older women in the office. These were the most difficult for me. From my first day of employment, I knew there was a group of women who resented the fact that I'd been hired. Each of them had been interested in the job I had been appointed to, and had bid for it as part of the internal search process. When none of them met the qualifications for the position, an external search was undertaken. I was fortunate enough to be recruited and got the position as the Community Outreach Specialist.

I was, however, deemed an "outsider" and treated accordingly. On my third day at work, I received an unexpected welcome from several of the women. I was in a stall in the ladies' room when I overheard three women talking about me. They were eagerly discussing their opinions of me, questioning my qualifications and speculating on whom I had slept with to get my job. The names of several men were suggested. I listened intently for a few minutes before exiting the stall. By the looks on their faces, they were shocked to see me. I strolled to the sink and soaped up my hands. I tried to still my emotions. I looked into the mirror and saw each of their reflections staring back at me. I smiled politely, turned off the faucet, and reached for some paper towels to dry my hands. It was then that I spoke.

"My qualifications for this position far exceeded any of the other candidates who submitted an application," I explained calmly. "I have fourteen years' experience in law enforcement, six of which were in management. By all accounts, no other candidate could match my credentials, training, and experience. And while each of you may have slept your way to the top, don't make assumptions about my behavior based on yours. I don't play where I work."

As I turned to walk away, I added one last comment.

"By the way, based on this incident, each of you has chosen the wrong profession. You don't belong in law enforcement. I would have made sure the person I was gossiping about was not present in the room. Next time, check the stall before you open your mouths."

I walked out of the bathroom and made a beeline to my boss's office. I told him about the incident in the ladies' room, and he listened intently.

When I was done speaking, the first thing he said was, "What am I, chopped liver? How come I'm not on that list of men you have slept with?"

I looked at him in disbelief, not getting the joke.

"I was trying to add some levity to the situation," he said. "Are you all right? Do you want me to talk with the women?"

"I'm fine. I don't need anyone to fight my battles, especially not you," I said. "If you interceded, they would add you to the list of suspected lovers."

I left his office wondering what had I done by taking this job. When I made the decision to accept the FBI's offer of employment, I thought I'd find a higher standard of behavior. After all, the Bureau represents itself as the premier law enforcement agency in the country. But those initial days indicated otherwise. It seemed that the FBI operated on the same level as the other agencies I had worked for. It left me wondering about my choice.

In the past, I'd had strained relationships with other women, but it was generally related to my position as a police officer. Not many women chose law enforcement as a profession back then. So, in general, I found that I had very little in common with other females. Even the older women in my family had a tough time comprehending why I would want to be a cop. And when I began working at the police department, the officers' wives also expressed resentment about my close working relationship with their husbands. Over time, however, many of the wives came to change their opinions and became more comfortable with me. Some of them even became my friends.

I didn't hear anything more about the incident in the ladies' room for some time. But later on one of the women who had been there came to me and explained the reasons behind her resentment and that of the other women. She explained that it had much to do with the past precedent of promotions within the Bureau. It seemed that, from the earliest history of the FBI, promotions had been handled primarily from within. Longevity of employment mattered more than specialized skills. But the present administration at FBI headquarters had begun a new hiring practice. All candidates were required to meet a new standard, including education, training, practical experience, knowledge, skills, and abilities. This shift had caused a great stir within the Bureau. With no way to argue with the policy makers, negative feelings in our office seemed to be directed at me. This woman went on to elaborate that there was additional resentment because of my entry-grade level and base pay. She also couldn't wait to relate that she and others in the office had bestowed the nickname of "slagent" when referring to me, a name given to describe my position. It seemed there were many questions regarding what my duties and responsibilities included. When described to any interested party, I was placed in this new category of employees who had job descriptions that were both support and agent in nature. I was branded with the new title and wasn't quite sure how to respond to it. Over the years to come, it was a nickname used by some of the employees in the office. And I was never quite sure whether it was supposed to be vindictive or complimentary.

So on the day I received the package from my former colleague, I was both excited and hesitant. I had not heard from her for a few months; she had not called to inquire about the state of my health or even to catch up. Her lack of interest in my well-being had hurt my feelings. I had thought of her quite often and had made two telephone calls to the office in hopes of hearing her voice. Just a couple of days before, I had lamented to a family member that I was upset because I had not heard from my friend.

With the arrival of the package, my mood changed. To my surprise, inside the plain brown box I found a lovely prayer shawl. The fabric was pale blue, green, and lavender with a smidgen of ivory. It was soft to the touch and intricately woven. As I unwrapped the beautiful piece, I found a kind note from my friend wishing me a speedy recovery. She explained that the shawl had been knitted by her and the other members of her congregation while they all prayed for me. As I read the note, my eyes filled with tears. I felt so relieved to know that my colleague truly cared about me and my return to health. I held the shawl close to my heart and said a prayer for the blessing of my friend and for her honorable intentions on my behalf.

A few nights later, I wasn't feeling very well. I had pain in my neck, arms, and hands. The tingling sensation in my right hand in particular was causing discomfort. As I prepared to go to bed, I placed the shawl around my shoulders. Almost immediately I felt heat in the middle of my back. The warmest sensation began running across my shoulders and down both of my arms. I felt a deep sense of comfort. It was as if I could feel the energy contained inside the shawl magically intertwine with mine. It seemed that each of the interlocking weaves held a prayer spoken on my behalf. I could hear the whispers of each voice that had invoked God to help me heal. I could almost see the women in the picturesque church as they knitted and shared pleasantries with one another. I could feel each finger as it delicately placed the yarn around the needle and pulled a stitch into place. As I ran my hand down the multicolored, softly woven tapestry, my mind relaxed and opened up to the concept of healing. Within a few moments, I fell asleep on my bed.

As I slept, I dreamed of the field and its angels. I was carried back to the scene of my arrival at the Flight 93 crash site. I saw the line of angels surrounding the plane, and I saw a darkness on the ground at their feet. All at once, the darkness turned to bright red and started to swirl in a violent pattern. The red color twisted into a tightly bound cylinder, like the shape of a tornado. The shape continued to morph until I could see that it was a demon. I saw its evil face with its deep, soulless eyes. I saw its terrible features of torment. The form twisted in great fury and gave a mighty roar. With its mouth gaping open, it then moved in a swift pattern across the ground. I felt the sensation of its breath upon my brow. My ears rang with the loudness of its voice. I awoke in great fear for my safety. I called out to Archangel Michael for his help.

As I yelled out Michael's name, I saw the image of Jesus rising from his tomb. He was draped in loosely fitting white garb that flowed as he moved across the ground. His arm was raised to the sky, and he was carrying a banner that bore a cross on it. As Jesus moved toward the demon, He stopped and stood directly above him. Jesus said nothing; He merely stayed in place awaiting the next move. This next move came in the beckoning of His angels.

I saw a shimmer of pale-pink light appear and begin to take form. The pink formation moved and began to grow and expand in its size. As a set of wings appeared, I heard the words, "Ariel has arrived."

Ariel did appear and took her position behind Jesus—as did Michael and the rest of the angels. They all moved in line behind her. Ariel began to move in the direction of the devil, swirling her lovely form straight toward him. As the two clashed, I again heard words being spoken.

"It is the final battle of good and evil. On this sacred ground, all that is good will conquer all that is evil. In this place, it will be done."

As these words were uttered, I saw the most amazing burst of light. As the light faded, I saw that the image of the demon was gone. All that was left in the place where he once stood was the softest white light.

When I awoke from this dream, I couldn't help but wonder about the deeper meaning of the events that took place on 9/11. I understood the importance of the battle between good and evil, and I also believed that this battle was a part of the events at the crash site. In the first moments of seeing the demon rising from the ground, I had been terrified. I had awakened to hear myself calling to Michael. He swiftly responded to my cries for help, bringing with him the lovely Ariel. As I remembered the warm sensation of my protector's arrival, I recalled that Ariel is also an archangel—the archangel of strength and courage. Ariel is the angel who is called upon in a time of need to bolster one's strength. She is often depicted as a lioness. On this night of my descent into the path of evil, she roared at the formations of evil and drove them back into their dark domain.

I found myself asking what else was meant by the presence of this darkness. I intuited that there was a hidden meaning, as my dreams often contain the answers to my questions. I spent time contemplating the underlying meaning of this dream over the next few days. I came to believe that the devil symbolized my fear of the personal demon I had been struggling with—PTSD. The fury of the demon depicted the wrath I was feeling inside. I was angry at myself for failing by becoming ill. I had failed those I loved, those I served, and myself. As human beings we struggle with the good and evil in ourselves and others. Like those others, my life has been represented by the image of an angel on one shoulder telling me to do good and the demon on the other shoulder telling me to be malicious. It was in this moment that I realized the demon was indeed symbolic of the fears that menaced my body and mind. I had fallen into a great abyss of anxiety and had buried myself in its deep dark hole. Just like the battle depicted on the field, I had been engaged in a struggle as well.

The next morning, I awoke to find the shawl still tightly wrapped around me. As I sat up in bed, I noticed the pain was gone. For ten days, I had suffered with the tightness in my neck and back and the tingling in my arms and hands. All that had dissipated during the night. During that Christmas season, I had been fortunate to receive yet another gift to enhance my already blessed life. The shawl had been sent to aid me in my healing. It was from someone who also shared my belief in God and His mercy. I hoped that someday I would be able to return her kindness and offer her a Christmas present of equal magnitude. In the meantime, I would say a silent prayer for her safekeeping.

CHAPTER
27

THE RETURN OF
AN OLD PATTERN

Shortly after the beginning of the new year, I returned to my weekly scheduled visits with the psychologist. As part of my weekly sessions, we incorporated a new type of therapy called "Heart Math," which is used to synchronize the electronics of the heart to help alleviate anxiety. The name Heart Math did not resonate well with me at first. I had a tough time believing that it could work. But as I thought more about it, I knew the resistance was just my ego. It was the same ego with which I had wrestled for so long. I thought that it had disappeared in my final recognition of the PTSD diagnosis and the exit of my superwoman persona. Unfortunately, it hadn't gone away. It merely lay in wait for the right opportunity to pounce again.

In February 2009, I sat describing my feelings—my disappointment at not moving forward in my healing. I told my therapist that I believed there was still a part of my brain that was congested. I explained about the headaches that plagued me and how I could feel a blockage in the lower left side of my head. We discussed my thoughts about what might be causing the congestion. I had no answer. With my reply, the psychologist began the session. She asked me the routine introductory questions, and I placed myself once again on the hill above the beaches of southwestern Ireland. This visualization is used to find a safe place to go if the patient becomes too distressed during the session. I chose this part of Ireland because it is my favorite location in the world—and the place where my spirit belongs.

In seconds, my mind opened up to an unfamiliar scene. I could see the inner spaces of my brain, with all its gray matter woven in miraculous turns. As my eyes traveled through the narrow passages of my brain, I became transfixed by a red color at the left base area. This section appeared to be inflamed and pulsing much more quickly than the other areas. It looked raw and angry. As I tried to look more closely at the area, my eyes shifted and my mind again traveled to the vision of the angels on the desolate field. I could hear the angels whispering to me that the lower corridor of my brain still burns red. It is red with leftover feelings of regret and my inability to forgive myself. I had not pardoned myself for the feelings that had momentarily incapacitated me at the site. I had not accepted the fear within me. In the lower left area of my brain, I was holding on to feelings of inadequacy and powerlessness. I also saw that I had sensed something negative was about to happen before September 11th. I had felt a foreboding similar to what I felt so many years ago as I patrolled the streets as a police officer.

Buried in this dark corner of my mind, I felt guilty for not having prevented the events of 9/11.

As I looked into the shadowy red area of my mind, I heard Michael's words once again. This time, they were intended for me.

"Move forward in God's design," he said. "Quit holding on out of fear and the lack of redemption for yourself. Place yourself back into the hands of God. Your blessings and gifts must not be hidden. The people in your life for the next three months are here to guide and protect you. The self-protection you seek is not necessary. The hand of God touches you and provides you with a gateway. You must practice your craft on a daily basis. I promise, all will make sense and all will be true. Keep the faith as the rest of the channels open. Those that came before you are also protecting you, and I never leave. In God's name, I say to you *let go*. Your path lies before you now."

A lovely and vibrant cobalt blue light flashed in front of my mind's eye. I felt peaceful and my mind calmed, quieted by the effect of Archangel Michael's words and their meaning. I was enlightened by his message, knowing that I am interconnected with everything.

I still awaken in the darkness on many nights and revel in the knowledge of his message. How exquisite the language, how pure the content. In the stillness of the night his meaning resonates to the deepest parts of my soul, and I wonder about the implications for us all.

CHAPTER
28

EMDR THERAPY

In June 2008, my journey to healing took another turn in the road. After months and months of conventional therapy, I was frustrated. I had not made the headway I had expected. I was stalemated by anxiety and the continued flashbacks of the field. I was desperate for any possible relief from the emotional and physical pain.

Around that time I had a conversation with a man who had once been my boss at the FBI. This man was someone I had grown to respect. Since his retirement from the Bureau, he had become a close friend and confidante. During our discussion, I told him about my concerns that my current therapy sessions didn't seem to be helping me. I explained how I felt like I was spinning in circles, sinking deeper into the thick murk of the memories with no real progress. As we spoke, he suggested that I ask my psychologist about a therapy known as Eye Movement Desensitization Repro-cessing (EMDR).

He explained that EMDR had been used for many years to aid military personnel and law enforcement officers who had been exposed to traumatic events in the line of duty. He even shared a personal story. He had used EMDR after an incident when he was a supervisory agent in Puerto Rico. He had been involved with an undercover investigation during which one of his colleagues had been murdered. He described in vivid detail the events that had led up to his involvement in the investigation, the shooting, the funeral, and his ultimate decision to engage in EMDR.

As he finished his story, I found myself crying. I could hear the emotion in his voice, too. Despite the years since the actual event, he was still deeply touched by the mem-ory of his fallen colleague. My heart ached for him. I was tearful over his loss. At the same time, I was relieved to encounter yet another strong and capable man whom I admired, who had openly admitted that at a time in his life, during a highly successful career, he'd needed help to restore his life. I can't describe the feeling of relief I had, knowing someone I respected understood how I felt. For too long, I'd felt isolated and distant. To hear his revelation reassured me that I was not alone.

His sharing stirred my intuition. I wanted to learn more about EMDR. All the therapy I'd been doing had not slowed the flashbacks. I was tired of the "hauntings," as my mind traveled to the same site time and time again. I feared the nighttime most, when I had to shut my eyes and dream about Shanksville. Each morning when I woke, it was still there before my eyes. So I was ready to try anything that might aid my healing.

A few days after our talk, it was time for my weekly visit to the therapist. After going through the routine checklist about my current health status—including the question I resented most (was I having suicidal or homicidal thoughts?)—I asked her what she knew about EMDR. She explained that EMDR was a powerful tool that can relieve many types of psychological distress. The EMDR therapist works with the patient to identify a specific problem as the focus of the treatment session. The patient is then requested to recall the disturbing memories, whether seen, heard, or felt. The therapist then instructs the patient to watch carefully as she moves her fingers up and down or side to side. The patient's eye movements simulate REM sleep, which is where many of our memories and experiences are processed. In the resulting hypnotic state, the patient may experience intense emotions that have lain dormant. Sometimes, the patient will recall additional information he or she had not remembered before. These remembrances may be the key elements keeping the patient from healing. Once these memories rise to the surface, the therapist is able to assist the patient in addressing the unresolved emotions.

My therapist concluded that EMDR would indeed be a good option for me to consider. Although the therapy would force me to remember the events of 9/11, it might help bring relief to the sharp images, smells, and sounds that had caused the traumatic effects to my psyche and heal the chronic health problems that plagued me.

As we finished our discussion, I asked if she would contact my primary care physician and the psychologist at the FBI to determine if EMDR therapy was a good choice for me and, if it was shown to be a good choice, whether there was a doctor trained in EMDR who could be recommended to treat me. In July of that year, I attended my first EMDR therapy session. My initial visit was filled with great anxiety and hesitation. But I felt that if EMDR was a proven method of treatment, I had little choice in the matter. I was ready to dig into the dark corners of my mind and relive the events that had wrought so much havoc in my life. It was time to deal directly with the ghosts that had haunted and immobilized me.

To my surprise, the EMDR sessions did more than just help me process the traumatic events of 9/11. They helped me expand my spirituality and gain a deeper understanding of my faith and my religious beliefs. As an added benefit, EMDR helped me begin to open to the intuitive gifts we all have. It seemed that mine had been blocked by all the memories of the field. As I cleared the sludge from my mind's clogged passageways, I found more and more clarity of insight. In the end, EMDR helped begin my path toward healing.

CHAPTER

29

LOOKING FOR A PIECE OF MYSELF

For all too many years now, the field of Shanksville on that fateful day has not left my mind's eye. The film repeatedly rewinds and plays back, time and time again. With each rewind, I see the vision of me, looking out over the expanse of the ground.

The scene has changed over time. The trees no longer hold horrific debris, and there are no more smells of burning pine or jet fuel. There are no more remnants of lives lost or things left undone, no more stolen moments of what could have been, and no last words to be said as the piper played the final note of his sullen melody. Now, I simply see myself standing there looking across the terrain.

As I stare into the distance on this "field of glory," my mind wanders to some deep abyss, to caverns and secret places. I wonder why I continue to stare at what is not there. Had I missed some detail all those years ago? Was there some task yet to do? Or was I still grieving the loss of life and the insanity of the deed? The answers to these questions came quite by surprise one warm September evening as I sat talking with a dear friend. As we spoke about life, the events of 9/11, the past years of ill health, and my inability to move forward, he offered a profound insight.

"You keep looking at the field to find *yourself*," he said. "You left some part of you on that field all those years ago and you keep waiting for her to return. She's out there. You just have to bring her back home."

When he finished speaking, I was flooded with emotion. It all began to make sense to me. Had I left so much of me behind on the field that I couldn't move forward into life in the present? As soon as he uttered those words, something inside me clicked. He was absolutely right. I had lost myself that day of September 11, 2001. The woman I had known for all my years had drifted away from me and had not yet returned. She had turned into a person who always seemed to be in "battle mode." Gone was the true essence of me. I had become a vigilant warrior, always watching, anxious for the bad tidings to come. The soft creature of my youth lay abandoned on that field. It was as if I had been kidnapped and held unwillingly in some unknown location.

As we sat and talked, I realized that this man fully understood my feelings. He "got me" and my thoughts. He was speaking from his own experience. He had served a tour of duty during the Vietnam War and once told me he hadn't come home the same person. He always felt that he was never quite right again. He understood all too well the "hauntings" and the sullen moods that crept up for no apparent reason. He had been an 18-year-old kid traveling to a place far from home, far from the comfort of his family and his friends, where he saw things no human being should ever witness.

He had left home a young man with hopes and dreams. He had come home a disillusioned man. He allowed no emotions to show. He was frozen in the memory of a life he'd left thousands of miles away.

To this day, when he speaks, I can still see a faraway look in his eyes. It tells me that he has once again traveled back to the place where he left his heart—and a piece of his sanity—so long ago. In a shared moment on my front porch that evening, I heard his heart beckon to me in full understanding.

Now, in the quiet stillness of this full moonlit night, came the knowledge of an answer I had sought for so long. All I needed to do was make the choice to return. When the next flashback of the field entered my mind, I would visualize myself turning around and walking away. I needed to say my good-byes, and walk back into this current life and my present reality. It was a solution that seemed to hold such promise for my recovery. I hoped my friend would take his own advice and walk back into his own life as well. Perhaps in time I could help him recover the soldier he, too, had left behind on his battlefield of long ago.

My mind is constantly besieged with thoughts of my next battle. It is unwavering in its design. It stands fast and ready as it waits for the next enemy to move across the horizon of my mind's refrain. I am battle prone in my stance. *Who might it be?* I hear inside my mind. I feel it in my body as the tension presses in on me. I see myself as the ever-vigilant warrior awaiting a foe who will allow me no quarter and no rest. The next round of destruction and pain is imprinted upon the recesses of my mind. I await an outcome with my pulse surging and my eyes intent on their next movement. If I waver, they may arrive unnoticed. If a reprisal is necessary, I must be prepared to strike back swiftly and with no mercy. The battle readiness remains as a perpetual part of my being. As one deluge passes, the other prepares to leap inside and take hold of the darkest parts of my brain. When will I just be at peace again? When will the fear, anxiety, and anger leave my tired brow? I stand isolated on this lonely field of glory just waiting for the next gladiator to appear.

RECONCILIATION OF MY MIND AND SOUL

It has now been more than a decade since 9/11. It has taken me this long to determine the appropriate time to share my story of God's field of angels. I do so now as a means of self-healing and reflection, for the greater good of His people, and as a way to move forward with my life. For these past few years, I felt as if my heart and mind were frozen in time. I have felt like a barren wasteland, unable to feel the warmth of the sun or the compassion of my heart. I have kept reliving those brief moments on that field in Shanksville when the angels first appeared and provided some hope to all of us who suffered on that September day.

Although others have experienced greater suffering than I did as a result of 9/11, I, too, have suffered many stressful days. I have continuously worried about how best to relate my tale to those willing to listen.

Even now, I share this story of the field of angels with mixed emotion. One side of me feels great joy at the prospect of sharing it with those who will believe. The other side of me is very hesitant. I hold my breath, awaiting the reaction of those who are most important to me. First there is my family, who already believes me to be slightly strange. Then there are my colleagues, whom I served alongside but with whom I somehow never quite fit in. Will they believe in what I witnessed? I wonder. Will they question my sanity?

At this point, however, I am sure of only one thing: it is time for others to know that there are angels walking this earth. That they wait in readiness to serve and protect. Angels are the kindred spirits of all of us in law enforcement and those of us who rise to the occasion as momentary heroes in response to life's terrible tragedies. They are guardians standing ready to protect us and defend us from harm. They are guides prepared to escort us on our journeys. They are healers who are ready to slay the most heinous of diseases. And, if we are fortunate, at the end of our lives, these angels will carry us back to the loving arms of God when He calls us home. Angels serve us and hear us when we cry to the Heavens for help. Just like that fall day in 2001 when the legion of angels carried the souls of our fallen heroes of Flight 93.

I can only pray that this story gives hope to those in despair, to those who still anguish over their losses and the sorrows in their lives. I have been blessed with "amazing grace," and now I wish to share it with others who need it. God is here. If we open our hearts and allow Him into our lives, He shares His love in the most unexpected moments. In our most troubling times, when we cry to Him for help, He sends the warmth of His heart to us. God sends us His guardian angels to serve, protect, guide, and heal.

The hardest part of the years since 9/11 has been the loneliness and isolation. In order to continue my path of self-protection, I had to keep from truly feeling or expressing my pain. I abandoned my need to extend myself to others. I denied myself many an opportunity to reach out for help. I expressed my feelings to only a select few immediate family members and close friends. Every choice I made, I did so only after a thorough analysis. I had to retain control of my feelings and thoughts in order to control the outcomes. I had to control all aspects of my life. I had to control my femininity and those natural instincts that make me a woman. I had to abandon my female intuition in order to survive. It was a role reversal. I let go of my naturally friendly demeanor, turning into a guarded and paranoid human being.

The pain and stress I felt came from my inability to forgive myself and the people in my past. The negative situations had faded, but the faces of those I had wronged and who had wronged me remained etched in my mind. The images had accumulated over the years. My karma had ripened and manifested as the illnesses that now plagued my body. I not only had physical pain, but my mind would not forgive my soul. My soul wailed inside, pleading for my mind to let go.

It was only in the final stages of digging into the buried pain that absolution and self-restoration began. I had to shovel through all the layers of the mud that had buried the real me. My life had lain dormant, unable to open up to the light. The return to the path of light lay in letting go of the pain. As I learned to just breathe, the layers of mud began to slowly dissolve. The murky waters began to clear. The shift was apparent. I now allowed myself to feel pain, and the pain provided an outlet to regain my voice. It was a voice that echoed and shared the stories of my past. My voice began to resonate with my soul.

My journey of spirituality began on that fateful day of 9/11. It continues with the release of my story and with the healing of my heart, mind, body, and soul. For it is only in the release of my story that emotional and physical healing can begin. In holding onto my story, I became sick with fatigue and anxiety. I have held it tight to my bosom like a protective mother ready to fight off any threat to her child. I have guarded it for far too long. Now I understand that the true essence of healing will come only with the release and the letting go. In order to heal and move forward, I must first dive into the recesses of my thoughts and feelings. I must allow myself to feel the remnants of the old in order to allow for the new. Knowing this, I now take my proverbial leap off of the cliff—praying that the net will appear.

CHAPTER
31

A SYMBOL OF RESURRECTION

When the airplanes hit the Twin Towers, the Pentagon, and the Shanksville landfill, the indescribable destruction that was left in their wake still remains a part of our daily lives in America. The aftermath of death and injury—and the pain of the survivors—remains with us to this day. America's once-confident stride was injured, and our trust in others was breached. Well over a decade later, remnants of the devastation remain, challenging our country's economy and many others as well.

However, out of the ashes of the ruins at each of these three sites rose symbols of our faith—reminding us that God was there on that September day.

As the mighty towers crashed to the ground in New York, a gesture of God's presence took shape in the abstraction of a large metal cross—not a manmade cross, but an image visible in the metal girders of the buildings at the base of Ground Zero. To those who looked at it daily, it brought hope for new life—and a possible future of reconciliation to all.

Many stories have now been written about that day—by survivors, responders, and victims' family members. Many have spoken of visits from beyond, and all are convinced their visions were real. Each describes the warm, loving feeling of being touched in this way. Whatever form the apparition took, it brought a sense of peace and comfort during a time of great grief.

At the Pentagon—a building designed to defend—structural damage was a constant reminder of the carnage that day. But some limestone was saved from the ruins, and crosses were built to symbolize death, rebirth, and new life. A cross was then gifted to each of the three crash sites. At the time of my medical leave, the cross gifted to the Pittsburgh Field Office stood in the corner of my office. It had been placed there by the man who had designed it. After it was exhibited for a short time in a local historical museum, my office had been its home since its arrival in Pittsburgh.

At the Shanksville landfill, God sent the gift of angels to remind us of His sustaining love. Out of the dark soot of the damaged landfill, the angels—and the souls of the faithfully departed—rose and moved toward God's light. This is my testimony of faith, hope, and love. It is a testament of the higher power that was seen not only by me but by others who sense its presence when they stand and walk on the hallowed ground of the field.

At each of these sites, there was recognition of God's omnipresence. He was present for those who died, for those who suffered, bore witness, responded and gave aid, and were raised to a level of heroism in death. For each person who played a role in this unfathomable event, God's grace was available. They say that bravery is only great when there is no hope. In those first few moments after the horrendous events, there seemed little to be hopeful about. Yet, as has been the case throughout human history, in our darkest times God has sent us all signs to bear witness of His kindness toward humanity.

Although the cross signifies great suffering to many of us, based upon our religious beliefs, it is also symbolic of God's promise for resurrection. And, in all the dark times of our country's history, the cross has been used as a sign of great hope to those who believe in life after death. In humanity's moment of extreme strife, humiliation, and pain, these symbols were offered to illuminate our path to recovery. Those who doubted God's presence on that fateful day received a sign of His deep love for us and His hope for our redemption. God gave us the message of the cross to remind us of His amazing grace and His belief in humanity's ability to prevail. On that day, there were signs of hope. It was a hope of survival and a reminder that we are all designed in the image of our Creator, each of us responsible one to the other.

EPILOGUE

Someday, in the distant future of time and space, long after the generations that survived the events of 9/11 are gone from their earthly domain, a small star will appear and shoot across the horizon. The star will shine down upon the field at Shanksville. As it shimmers in the night sky, children will look at it in wonder. Just like the storytellers from medieval times, these children's parents will "tell the tale" of the field of angels and the heroes of Flight 93. As the star twinkles in the darkness of the universe's indigo abyss, it will be a reminder of a great deed done—a deed completed to fulfill the purpose of many lives that moved all too swiftly from birth to death to rebirth. When this tiny light shoots across the vastness of the sky, so will the memories of these events lie limitless in the mind's eye. For courage and valor are the best human traits shared by those who perished on that plane.

AUTHOR'S
CLOSING NOTE

As this book comes to an end, I want to clarify an issue. I did not provide more in-depth information about the FBI because of bureau policy. In order to publish a book, a current or former employee must abide by policies mandated by the Bureau. The publication may not reveal any information that might be considered "classified" or "sensitive" in nature. In order to meet the standard of this policy, I have kept the FBI-related information in a generic form. So if I have left any questions unanswered, I apologize and ask that you understand the constraints of my former employment.

The opinions expressed in these chapters are those of Lillie Leonardi and not of the FBI.

ACKNOWLEDGMENTS

To my daughter and grandchildren, you are my heart's content.

To my Mother, you gave me the courage to move forward.

To my brother Sam, you encouraged me to pursue my dreams.

To my dearest friends; Bill, Connie, Judy, Lisa, Michele, Pierina, Raymond, Stacy and Terri for supporting my dream.

To the Agency Representatives who responded to the Flight 93 crash site, for serving in the best interest of your fellow man.

To the members of the United Airlines Humanitarian Response Team, for the compassion shown to the victims and families of Flight 93.

To my literary agent Cynthia Cannell, for having the faith to represent a novice author.

To my editor Patty Gift, for your belief in this story.

And to Cally, for all of your tireless efforts in making this book possible.

ABOUT THE AUTHOR

Following her 25-year career of service in law enforcement, Lillie Leonardi is pursuing her lifelong passion for writing.

From 1998 to 2010, Lillie Leonardi was employed by the Federal Bureau of Investigation (FBI), Pittsburgh Division, as its Community Outreach Specialist. Leonardi's work and research focused on violence prevention. She also served as a training instructor under the auspices of the United States Attorney's Office, Western District of Pennsylvania.

On September 11, 2001, immediately following the crash of Flight 93 in Shanksville, Pennsylvania, Leonardi was deployed to the crash site, where she would spend the next 12 days. During that time, she was tasked to serve as the primary liaison with law enforcement, government, and human service entities, including the United Airlines humanitarian response team. She also assisted in the coordination of the two memorial services.

Post-9/11, Leonardi represented the FBI in collaboration on three projects relating to Flight 93: with the Smithsonian Institute, with the Senator John Heinz History Center, and with the Flight 93 Oral History Project, coordinated by the Department of the Interior.

Prior to her career with the FBI, in 1984, Leonardi was appointed to serve as the first female police officer with the City of Arnold, Pennsylvania. While employed with the police department, she specialized in crime prevention and investigations of crimes against children. This is Leonardi's first book.

www.lillieleonardi.com

Hay House Titles of Related Interest

All of the above are available at your local bookstore,
or may be ordered by contacting Hay House (see next page).

⟞⟝

We hope you enjoyed this Hay House book. If you'd like
to receive our online catalogue featuring additional information
on Hay House books and products, or if you'd like to find out
more about the Hay Foundation, please contact:

Hay House UK, Ltd., 292B Kensal Rd., London W10 5BE
Phone: 0-20-8962-1230 • *Fax:* 0-20-8962-1239 •
www.hayhouse.co.uk • **www.hayfoundation.org**

✥

Published and distributed in the United States by:
Hay House, Inc., P.O. Box 5100, Carlsbad, CA 92018-5100
Phone: (760) 431-7695 or (800) 654-5126
Fax: (760) 431-6948 or (800) 650-5115
www.hayhouse.com®

Published and distributed In Australia by: Hay House Australia Pty. Ltd.,
18/36 Ralph St., Alexandria NSW 2015 • *Phone:* 612-9669-4299 • *Fax:*
612-9669-4144 • www.hayhouse.com.au

Published and distributed in the Republic of South Africa by:
Hay House SA (Pty), Ltd., P.O. Box 990, Witkoppen 2068
Phone/Fax: 27-11-467-8904 • www.hayhouse.co.za

Published in India by: Hay House Publishers India, Muskaan Complex,
Plot No. 3, B-2, Vasant Kunj, New Delhi 110 070 • *Phone:* 91-11-4176-
1620 • *Fax:* 91-11-4176-1630 • www.hayhouse.co.in

Distributed in Canada by: Raincoast, 9050 Shaughnessy St., Vancouver,
B.C. V6P 6E5 • *Phone:* (604) 323-7100
Fax: (604) 323-2600 • www.raincoast.com

✥

Take Your Soul on a Vacation

Visit **www.HealYourLife.com®** to regroup, recharge,
and reconnect with your own magnificence.
Featuring blogs, mind-body-spirit news, and life-changing
wisdom from Louise Hay and friends.

Visit **www.HealYourLife.com** today!

JOIN THE HAY HOUSE FAMILY

As the leading self-help, mind, body and spirit publisher in the UK, we'd like to welcome you to our family so that you can enjoy all the benefits our website has to offer.

 EXTRACTS from a selection of your favourite author titles

 **COMPETITIONS, PRIZES & SPECIAL OFFERS** Win extracts, money off, downloads and so much more

 LISTEN to a range of radio interviews and our latest audio publications

 **CELEBRATE YOUR BIRTHDAY** An inspiring gift will be sent your way

 **LATEST NEWS** Keep up with the latest news from and about our authors

 ATTEND OUR AUTHOR EVENTS Be the first to hear about our author events

 iPHONE APPS Download your favourite app for your iPhone

 **HAY HOUSE INFORMATION** Ask us anything, all enquiries answered

join us online at **www.hayhouse.co.uk**

 292B Kensal Road, London W10 5BE
T: 020 8962 1230 E: info@hayhouse.co.uk